the River of
GRACE

a story of John Calvin

To my husband, Garth

*"Faith and hope are the wings by which our souls,
rising above the world, are lifted up to God."*

Greenleaf Press
3761 Hwy 109 North, Lebanon, TN 37087
www.greenleafpress.com

the River of
GRACE

a story of John Calvin

by Joyce McPherson

Greenleaf Press
Lebanon, Tennessee

TABLE OF CONTENTS

Deus vult
(God wills it)

~Motto of the Crusades

1
A CHRISTIAN SOLDIER
1517

John brandished his stick in the air. "I am Sir John and I declare that I will go on a pilgrimage to the Holy City." He looked fiercely into the summer sun as he imagined a brave knight would.

He did not look much like a knight. He was small for his seven years and wore the plain breeches and tunic of a school boy. Nevertheless, he did look brave. His brown eyes flashed fire and he firmly clasped his sword to his side.

John bowed his head and made the sign of the cross. His friend, Claude, knelt at his feet.

"I will follow my lord wherever he goes," Claude announced solemnly. He liked to say "my lord," because it sounded official. He often heard it in his own home where his father received tenant farmers. They called him "my lord."

John swung his leg over a stone wall which served as his horse. His friend mounted behind him, and they began their journey.

"We must face severe trials," John said after a short pause.

"Will there be Turks?" asked Claude.

"Yes, and bandits, too. We will fight them and claim all their treasure for the Church and Pope Leo the Tenth."

"And Pope Leo will reward us," added Claude.

"Yes, when we arrive at the Holy City, we will see him wearing his triple crowns. When we give him the treasure, he will bless us and forgive all our sins."

Suddenly, John jumped from his horse. "What is this heresy that I see?"

Claude looked at the hens pecking in the dirt nearby. "I don't see anything."

John shook his stick impatiently. "Heresy is anything against Mother Church, and those hens are a pack of rascally heretics who are trying to lead the people away from Mother Church."

"Let us scatter them!" cried Claude.

John waved his stick and shouted while Claude stomped menacingly. The hens flitted to a safer spot a few yards away.

John made an eloquent bow. "You put the knaves to flight and saved me when the enemy pressed around me. I owe to you my life and whatever I have."

Claude bowed in return. "I only do my duty," he

replied stiffly.

John stooped to pick up a round stone. "Look at this, Sir Claude. This is a rock that was thrown at Saint Stephen when he was killed."

"A relic," said Claude reverently. "It has special powers to protect from demons."

"This is a good omen," said John. He climbed nimbly onto his horse just as the sound of the cathedral bells interrupted their pilgrimage.

John's mother claimed that the bells were saying, "If you waste your bread you'll get a rap on the head!"

The bells reminded John that he did not want to be late for dinner. "It is six bells. I have to go home," he said.

"But you still have time to play. The cathedral bells are always the first to ring. You will not be late until all the bells have finished ringing."

"Papa says I must come home when the cathedral bells ring," said John.

Claude insisted they take a sacred oath to continue in the service of France and the King before they went home.

John clasped hands with his friend. "We are Christian soldiers," he declared. He did not know exactly what the words meant, but he had heard his older cousin, Pierre, mention the Christian soldier and something about a man named Erasmus.

The boys brandished their sticks in the air one last time. Claude shouted, "I'll see you tomorrow

JOHN RUNS HOME

morning for lessons! The tutor says he will teach us horseback riding if we are good students!"

4

John wanted to whoop for joy, but he knew that a knight would never do that. Instead, he saluted smartly before he ran for home.

All around him the bells of other churches floated on the evening breeze. John passed the Cathedral and the cluster of clerics' homes that surrounded it. People called it "the city within the city of Noyon." There were dozens of priests and monks who lived and worked there. It was also the headquarters of the Bishop of Noyon, who was Claude's uncle.

John ran past the back of a row of town houses. Each house had its own garden. He waved to neighbors who were busily tending their gardens.

John rounded a corner and almost collided with a pig that was wandering in the narrow side street. "Get home," he urged the pig as he gave it an affectionate pat. There was no time to return it to the neighbor's yard today, but the pig had not strayed too far. As the last of the church bells finished ringing, John arrived on the Wheat Market square where the sun glinted on the greenish glass windows of his home. He took the stairs two at a time and arrived breathless in the doorway.

The Calvin home was simply furnished. A wooden table, worn smooth from generations of Calvins, filled the main room. A round white pitcher stood on a shelf. In the corner lay the cradle for baby François.

Papa looked up from the thick floury soup that

he was eating and nodded to John. "I was wondering if I would have someone to eat with. The baby is asleep and your little brother has already finished his dinner. Your mother is putting him to bed."

"I'm sorry I'm late for dinner," John began.

Papa noted his disheveled clothing and frowned in mock concern. "Doesn't your tutor require more than play in the afternoons?"

"I wrote all my lessons before we played," explained John.

"They must not give you many lessons," said Papa. "When I was a student in 1490, we worked much harder because books were not as common as they are today."

John slid onto a bench and waited expectantly for his father to finish. He knew that he must not eat until he had made the sign of the cross and prayed over his food.

Papa continued, "We had to make our own books. We wrote as fast as we could while our teacher dictated the lessons from his tall wooden chair. How many manuscripts do you think we had in our town?"

John, who had been staring hungrily at the large pot of soup, sat up straight and looked at his father. "I will guess ten," he replied with a firm voice in the way Papa had taught him.

His father nodded approvingly. "That is a good guess since you are blessed to live in Noyon which has an entire church library. But our little town had only one manuscript! The monks chained it to the lectern in the abbey. We could only learn as much as our teacher could dictate to us."

Papa bit from a large slice of bread and chewed it thoughtfully while John tried not to think of food. "You should be thankful, John, that you can learn so many things from books now. You can buy a grammar book for Latin or Greek, or even Hebrew, and teach yourself all the wisdom of the ancients." Papa nodded to signal that he was done. "You may eat now, John."

John said a hasty prayer and ladled the soup into his bowl. He was silent for several minutes while he savored the thick soup.

Papa did not allow children to talk at meals unless they had an important question, but John already had a question in mind. "Papa, what is a Christian soldier?"

"Did you hear this from your cousin, Pierre?" he asked.

John flushed. He wondered if he had said something wrong. "Yes sir. He told me he was a Christian soldier like someone named Erasmus."

Papa scowled. "You come from a good home, John. You must not fill your head with such things. The priests at the Cathedral say Erasmus is a dangerous man. He is trying to get part of the Bible printed in the original language, and the priests say there is no end to the trouble that might befall us if the Holy Word is read by any fool who finds a copy of it. I have told your cousin many times that he must leave such things alone."

John wanted to ask more questions, but from the look on Papa's face, he knew he should remain silent. He finished dinner quickly and slipped into the bedroom that he shared with his little brother. Antoine slept peacefully. John decided it was better to be like Antoine and not have so many questions. Thoughts of Christian soldiers drifted through his mind, and he slept.

Time reveals all things.

~Erasmus

2

GREAT AND LONG ROADS

John gripped his quill pen and carefully scratched letters onto the parchment. Light brown hair curled in thin wisps around his face. His brown eyes clouded in concentration. He stopped for a moment to survey his work. He looked at each letter in turn, as though it was an unruly school child who might break out of the straight lines at any moment. Was the curlicue on the *T* just right?

"John, where are you?" a woman's voice called.

"Here, Mama." He quickly penned the year "1518" under his name, then gently sprinkled the parchment with sand and slipped it under his cot.

The door opened and a cheerful face appeared from behind the door. John's own mother had died when he was three years old. His father had married this petite woman with dark brown hair. She had become "Mama" to John and his brothers. She had a wide mouth and arched eyebrows that made her look as though she had just finished laughing. "Where have you been all afternoon?" she asked.

"Just here," John answered simply. He hoped she would not ask any more questions.

His mother noted the ink stains on his fingers and nodded her head. "You have been writing, I see. You are fortunate to be able to learn these things, and only nine years old, too. You must teach your little brother everything you learn."

John's face brightened at her words. "Yes, Mama. I will teach Antoine. There is so much to learn at our new school. Our professor at the College of Capettes knows even more than Claude's tutor. He has started us in Latin. Would you like to hear some?"

John did not wait for his mother's reply. He stood and quoted enthusiastically, "'*Magnae et longae viae.*' That means, 'great and long roads.' I can write it for you, too."

John stopped as he suddenly remembered the piece of parchment hidden under his cot. "Well, maybe later when Papa is here." John felt his face turning red. He could not keep secrets from Mama. At that moment a soft whistle sounded from outside the house. "It's Pierre! May I go out and see what he wants?"

Mama shook her head in mock wonder. "John, you are going in so many directions at once! Writing things, speaking Latin, seeing your friends. You will have to slow down one day. Go see your cousin, but make sure you are back for dinner!"

John gave his mother a quick hug and raced out the door. It was a rare treat to spend time with Pierre, and he couldn't waste a moment of it. His cousin stood next to a shop near John's house. He was a sturdy young man of fifteen. He stared nonchalantly at the stout oak door of the shop, as though it were his only reason for being on this street at this hour of the afternoon. When John greeted him, Pierre turned and gave his entire attention to the younger boy. "How have you been?" he asked.

"I have been studying Latin since I saw you last," John responded. He hoped Pierre would be impressed.

Pierre nodded gravely. "That is a good thing. It will prepare you to be a Christian soldier."

"But Papa wants me to study to be a priest," John replied.

Pierre laughed. "Anyone can be a Christian soldier, even priests. It means that you follow Christ. Erasmus says that even the farmer at his plow should ponder God's Word while he works. But first he must be able to read it."

John gasped. "Read God's Holy Bible? How could he do that?"

Pierre put his hand on John's shoulder. "That is why I have come to see you," he said, his eyes taking on a fierce intensity. "I will be leaving for the Sorbonne University tomorrow. I will learn to read the Bible there! Just think of it, John. Today I am a simple scholar from Noyon, but tomorrow I will be a university student."

John stared at Pierre. He could not think what to say. Even his older brother, Charles, who was a priest, had never been to the Sorbonne University. The afternoon sun slipped behind a cloud, and John suddenly felt cold. He knew Pierre longed to go to the university, but at this moment it seemed very far away in a very big world.

Pierre continued. "I will tell you all about it when I visit my parents. And one day you must come, too."

A sudden desire welled up inside of John. He squared his shoulders in emulation of Pierre's strong stature. "I will come," he promised.

Pierre smiled and clapped John on the back. "Good," he replied, "Until then!"

John watched him walk down the cobbled street until he disappeared from sight around the corner. He would have a lot to tell Papa at dinner tonight, but first he would take a walk and think about things.

John turned towards the great cathedral that towered above the houses of Noyon. From his home John could see the bulky outline of the two main towers pointed straight up to Heaven. It was the oldest gothic cathedral in France and the pride of the citizens of Noyon.

John followed the old Roman road that led him to the foot of the grand cathedral. He lingered at the edge of the square while monks and priests strode purposefully through the cathedral doors. Around the stone towers pigeons flocked. John liked to imagine that it was seven hundred and fifty years ago when

JOHN LOOKS UP AT THE CATHEDRAL

the Bishop of Noyon crowned the great Charlemagne
on this site. Men had not yet built the great
cathedral in those days.

John tilted back his head to see the top of the

cathedral. He wondered about the men who had built it. How did they know how to fit the stones together and make the arches so that they would not fall? How did they learn to sculpt the stone so ornately? There were so many things that John wanted to know, but he barely knew where to begin. His teachers kept reminding him that the road to knowledge began with the little lessons he was learning now. John took a deep breath, as though to drink in the beauty of the cathedral once more, then he turned to go. As he walked back to his house, his Latin lesson echoed in his mind, *"Magnae et longae viae, magnae et longae viae*, great and long roads . . ."

John entered the house to find his brother, Charles, home for a visit. He was in heated discussion with John's father. Papa's hearty voice boomed against the walls. "That is the problem with the Cardinal . . ." He stopped in mid-sentence as John entered the room.

John pretended that he did not hear the conversation. Their home also served as his father's office, and Papa did not approve of children listening to adult conversations. John bowed politely to his father, and Papa motioned with a large sweep of his hand for John to sit on the bench next to him. John waited for him to speak first.

Papa smiled and began, "I heard that you have begun to study Latin."

John nodded enthusiastically. "Yes! Pierre says it is a good thing to study." John felt his cheeks begin to burn as he said shyly, "I have something for you,

14

Papa." Without waiting for an answer he ran up the steps to the little room that served as bedroom for Antoine and himself. John found the parchment that he had hidden under his cot. He returned to his father. "This is for you, to show what I am learning at school."

John's father studied the parchment for a moment, then slapped his leg and laughed. "You are an eager student. I must talk to the Bishop about getting you a clerical post! It will earn enough money to give my eager student a good education." He laughed again, as though it were a good joke.

Charles did not laugh. He rose stiffly. "I must take my leave." He turned to John. "I am proud of your hard work. I hope with all my heart that Papa will see the good sense of sending you to Paris and not . . ." He stopped abruptly and quickly left the house.

Papa looked thoughtful. "Your brother has many cares, John. He wants me to make plans for your future. He thinks you must go to the Sorbonne University one day. I will have to talk to the Bishop about this."

John hardly listened to the rest of his father's words. His heart thumped hard in his chest. The university? Papa wanted him to go there? John found his voice. "I really *do* want to go to the university, Papa."

Papa leaned close to John and suddenly became serious. "John, going to the universtiy means hard work. Do you understand what that means?"

John swallowed hard and nodded his head.

Papa continued. "Your grandfather worked hard making barrels. He began as an apprentice in the Cooper's Guild. Do you know what he had to learn?"

"No, Sir."

"He had to learn to cut oak into staves that were just the right thickness. He worked for a master cooper for many years and learned to do it perfectly. Then, he was allowed to learn how to heat and steam the staves so that they could be bent into shape. The master cooper taught him how to hammer iron hoops around the staves so that the barrels would not leak. He became a journeyman when he learned his trade. The cooper paid him for his work and he could afford to marry. Do you think your grandfather was a journeyman for the rest of his life?"

"No, Papa. You told me that he became a master cooper."

"That is correct. He saved his money so that he could pay the guild fee. The guild required him to prove that he could make airtight barrels. He worked hard to present his finely made barrels to the guild. These barrels were called his masterpiece. Your grandfather became a master cooper because he worked hard. He taught me to work hard, too. I studied hard in school, and now I am the attorney to the Bishop!" He struck his chest with his hand as he pronounced the last statement.

John swelled with pride that his father was such an important man. Perhaps he would grow up to be a man like his father.

Orare est laborare, laborare est orare
(To pray is to work, to work is to pray)

~Motto of the Benedictine Monks

3
A YOUNG CHAPLAIN

John awoke to the sound of bells. The room was icy cold. John hunched deeper under his warm covers and hoped it would be acceptable to say his prayers in bed rather than on his knees this morning. He could hear his mother singing softly in the kitchen. It must be time for breakfast.

John gritted his teeth and pulled on his shirt and coat which were stiff from the cold. He jumped down the steps two at a time, and ran to the kitchen fireplace where he had placed his boots the night before. They were smoking slightly. Mama scolded him for placing them too near the fire again.

"You'll burn the house down around our heads if you are not more careful," she said.

Papa was slicing a loaf of bread and grumbling about the baker. "The government regulates the price of bread, so the baker puts less and less wheat in the loaf." He held up a slab of the dense

17

bread. "The baker must have ground acorns and chestnuts with the grains to make this loaf!"

Mama lightly transferred a steaming pot to the table. "Gerard, you know the famine has made the cost of wheat too high this year. Be thankful for what the Lord has given you."

Papa winked at John and continued, "I'm only saying this for John's benefit. What if he were to eat something unholy that the baker put in the bread when no one was looking? What would become of the vows he is supposed to take today?"

Mama made the sign of the cross. "Where do you get your ideas? We do not need to worry, because John must observe a fast this morning." As the bells tolled the half hour, she pushed John out the door. "You go to the Bishop now," she told John. "We will see you at the Cathedral."

Several hours later, John took his place for the ceremony. Priests, in their canonical robes, led the procession. The smoke from their censors wreathed their heads and made them look holy. There were servants in uniforms to carry the Sacred Host. The Bishop wore a tall miter on his head. He walked stiffly behind the priests. Next came the choir boys in white robes. Their high voices sang a litany. John recognized the melody from the days when he was a choir boy.

At the front of the cathedral the Bishop nodded for John to come forward to the altar. John's head felt light. His feet moved mechanically, as though they did not belong to him.

The Bishop asked in his booming voice, "What is

THE PROCESSION

your wish?"

John swallowed and tried to make his voice match the Bishop's firmness. "To serve God and the Church."

The Bishop directed John to kneel. In the

flickering candlelight John saw the embroidered sleeve of the Bishop's robe as he placed his hand on John's head. He prayed for John in Latin. The choir sang a simple chant while the Bishop performed the Rite of Tonsure. He cut five pieces of hair from John's head. As John heard the scissors snip, he remembered what he had been told, "This is to separate each of my five senses from the world."

Bishop de Hangest asked, "What is your inheritance?"

John answered proudly, "The Lord is my inheritance." The Bishop prayed a solemn prayer in Latin.

John was now a chaplain of Mother Church.

ஐ ෬ ෪

John sat at the table and reverently smoothed the yellow page of a large book. He had borrowed it from the family library of his friend, Claude. He leaned his forehead against his hand as he bent over the book. He was so intent on his reading that he did not hear the murmur of voices from the next room where his father was meeting with some canons of the Church. The canons were priests who served in the Cathedral.

Beautiful letters on the cover of the book spelled *The Book of Hours*. Intricate borders and patterned bands decorated the pages. There were even some pictures made from woodcuts. John read the prayers and texts of church services. There was also a calendar and almanac.

Papa entered the room at the dinner hour. He pondered his son for a moment then spoke in a teasing voice. "John, you must stop your reading for a few minutes or I will not have a table for my dinner."

With a great effort John closed the book. He felt as though he had scarcely breathed all morning. There were so many riches to be mined from this book. It seemed a pity to have to stop for dinner. "Is it already time for dinner?" he asked.

Papa laughed. "You remind me of the scholars of your grandfather's day. There are stories of men who walked four hundred miles to be able to go to a school, and then they had to work in the kitchen to be allowed to stay. One student could only study at night after his work was done. He would climb to the top of the bell tower and read Latin by the light of the moon."

John looked at the yellowed page before him and imagined that he was curled up in a stone tower reading by moon light. "Did he ever graduate from that school?"

"Not only did he graduate, but he became the principal of the College de Montaigu, which is part of the Sorbonne University that you want to attend!"

John told himself he would study harder than ever, even if he had to study all night. He started to return to his reading, but Papa gently picked up the book and placed it on a shelf. "That is enough for any young person. You must feed your body, too." His voice held a note of wistfulness as he added, "If only the problems of our canons would occupy me as fully as your books, I would not be so eager for dinner. But my stomach has been rumbling all morning!"

A baby's cry interrupted their conversation. John went to the cradle by the wall and lifted out a well-bundled baby girl. She responded by crying louder. John gently rocked her and she quieted.

Papa nodded in approval. "It is good that you care for your sister now. Little Marie will grow up one day, but it will be your duty to care for her."

The baby clutched John's finger in her chubby fist. John tried to imagine Marie as a grown woman, but he could not do it.

At that moment she began to cry again, and John's mother swooped in and rescued the baby. She directed John to serve the "fasting meal" that she had prepared. Since it was Friday, there was no meat or butter in the meal.

"Have you heard from Pierre?" Papa asked John, as they sat down to eat dinner.

"Yes," John replied. "He is doing well, but he says he must study all the time. The other students have nicknamed him 'Olivétan.'"

"They call him Olivétan? That means 'Midnight Oil!'" Papa said with amusement. "He must be burning the midnight oil, working late into the night."

"Papa, when will I be able to attend the university?" asked John.

His father studied him for a long moment. "You certainly burn the midnight oil, but I don't think you are ready for the university yet. Besides, you are only twelve. Whoever heard of a boy attending the university so young? Pierre is brilliant, and he did not go until he was fifteen."

John knew there was no arguing with Papa.

That afternoon Mama asked John to accompany her to the cathedral for the evening Mass. John gave a longing glance toward his book, but he went with his mother. As they entered the cathedral, the somber quietness of the place descended on John. Thick incense filled the sanctuary. Along the walls, tapers glowed before the statues of saints. Mama made the sign of the cross and prayed to each one. In the holiness of the cathedral John forgot the book, Pierre, and even the university.

A dim recollection surfaced of a time when he was only three years old. John remembered walking a long, dusty road to a little shrine. His mother had reverently explained that this was a shrine to Saint Anne who was the grandmother of the Lord Jesus. John felt the excitement all over again as he thought of how his mother had lifted him up to kiss the gold box that held the skull of Saint Anne.

John thought, "Such holy things for a little child! Now I know so much more."

He knelt beside his mother, and began to recite the prayers his mother had taught him. Gradually his prayers quickened. He counted them quietly to himself. There, I've said the Lord's Prayer the right number of times. Now for the Hail Marys. He counted as he recited the prayer to the Virgin Mary over and over. There, done! His mother had already finished her prayers. She sat expectantly on the rough wooden bench for the priest to begin the Mass.

John sat next to her and waited, too. His eyes followed the decorated stones up to the high ceiling. The windows glimmered lightly.

At last the priest approached the alter. As his voice intoned the prescribed service in Latin, John tried to catch scraps of Latin that he could understand. The priest pronounced many of the words differently from John's teacher. John wished he could sneak up and peek at the Bible that the priest was using. It was one of the few Bibles in the town of Noyon. He wondered if there were more Bibles at the university. Of course, since he would be studying to be a clergyman, he would be able to look at a Bible one day.

Mama squeezed his hand as they solemnly walked from the cathedral. "Thank you for coming with me, John," she said. "You know we must never miss Mass. Something terrible might happen if we did." Mama shuddered. "And we have so much to be thankful for: a healthy baby, our good home."

John thought of baby Marie's chubby hands clutching his finger. He must remember to say some extra Hail Marys for his baby sister.

Cucullus non facit monachum
(The cowl does not make a monk)

~ Medieval proverb

4
THE LATIN QUARTER

John reined in his horse and took a last look at the towers of Noyon. Claude and his younger brother joined John. "It's going to be a lot different where we are going!" said Claude with enthusiasm.

Monsieur Courbet, who served as the guardian for the boys, said crisply, "In Paris there is a magnificent Cath-edral of Notre Dame, just as there is in Noyon. Perhaps you will find many things the same, Master Claude."

Claude pretended to groan. "I can't believe that Paris will be the same. It will be an adventure, just like the games we played when we were children."

"If I remember correctly, we were always going on pilgrimages," said John with a grin.

For an answer, Claude spurred on his horse. "Let's race to the crossroads!"

John urged his horse after him.

When the horses grew tired, Monsieur Courbet announced that it was time for lunch. He produced a packet with coarse bread and cheese.

Claude whispered to John, "Watch how I can make Monsieur Courbet turn red." He turned to the group and announced: "Ever since Martin Luther nailed his ninety-five theses to his church door, he has been making trouble. He says that people should pray to God and not to the Virgin Mary and the other saints."

Monsieur Courbet made a small choking sound as he swallowed his bread. "Excuse me, Master Claude, but this is not an appropriate topic for the sons of gentlemen."

Claude brashly continued. "We will be living in Paris. We can't be sheltered all our lives. Besides, a man named Ulrich Zwingli has been leading a reform in the Swiss city of Zurich for two years, and no one has stopped him."

John listened with interest. Papa did not allow him to discuss such issues at home.

Monsieur Courbet turned red. He fixed Claude with a severe look. "The Pope and the Sorbonne University have declared Luther to be a heretic, so we will not discuss this further."

Claude winked at John, but said nothing more.

Dusk was falling on the dark crenelated turrets of the city's wall as the weary travellers arrived on the outskirts of Paris. John saw the towers and spires of several churches which rose above gabled houses with their red tile roofs and square chimneys. Pigeons flocked among the stone towers of the churches.

John led his horse through the narrow crooked streets and muddy lanes to the center of the city. Papa had given him directions. He easily found the Louvre, which was the palace of King Francis. The king's standard, with the symbol of the salamander, flew proudly over the palace. The horsemen turned east and followed the walls of the huge building, which was built to honor the grandeur of the King.

Claude leaned from his horse. "We're really here!"

They followed the road until they reached the Place of the Greve. It was the place of execution. John shuddered at the sight of a pile of faggots that had been assembled for the next burning at the stake. Yes, we're really here, he thought grimly.

A narrow bridge spanned the Seine River a short distance from the Place of the Greve. The bridge connected with an island that stood in the middle of the river. Papa had told John about the island. It was called the Isle de la Cité and was the birthplace of Paris. John's horse crossed to the ancient island and brought John to the feet of an immense cathedral.

"That is the Cathedral of Notre Dame," said John in hushed tones. The three boys made the sign of the cross.

They crossed another bridge from the Isle de la Cité to the left bank of the Seine, where the

Sorbonne University was located.

"This is called the Latin Quarter because Latin is the language of all scholars," explained Monsieur Courbet.

John followed the winding streets to his Uncle Richard's blacksmith shop. Several buildings had large wooden doors. The de Hangests' guardian explained that the doors opened onto courtyards surrounded by several buildings. John paused to admire the iron tracery that decorated the houses. He momentarily forgot his weariness in his curiosity about the city that would be his home. Too soon Monsieur Courbet announced, "Master John, this is your uncle's home. We will leave you here and go to our lodgings."

John thanked Monsieur Courbet and bade his friends farewell.

John awoke to the silvery sound of the bells of the Church of Saint Germain. He did not know where he was at first. Then in a rush, he realized that he was in his uncle's house in Paris. He was a scholar at the Sorbonne University! Hastily he threw off his bed covers and dashed some water on his face. He knelt next to his bed and said a quick version of his usual prayers. He pulled on his gray college gown and cap, and scooped up the few books that he had.

His aunt greeted him as he entered the kitchen. She was a cheerful woman with gray hair that showed in wisps around the edges of her white cap. "I see you don't have time to eat, but take some of these rolls with you. A scholar needs nourishment, you know." John thanked her and hurried out to meet the de Hangest brothers at their lodging. They had decided to walk together to the university. Claude was not yet out of bed, and the young men barely made it to the chapel on time.

The quiet peacefulness of the church was a welcomed change after the initial rush to get to the chapel. John recited the rosary. He paid careful attention to all that the priest said. It was exciting to think that he was beginning his training for the clergy today. He said an extra prayer to the Holy Virgin to bless his preparation for the priesthood. After chapel, John went to the College de La Marche.

Two filthy houses on a courtyard comprised the College de La Marche. They were the language house and the literature house. The professors required the students to speak in Latin at all times.

The first day was a whirlwind of classes, assignments, and new routines. The students learned that they would begin class at five in the morning each day. They must bring their books, a candle, and a lapboard to class with them. At ten o'clock they would have a break for lunch and recreational reading. Then they must attend class from one until five again. John figured that he must rise at four each morning in order to say his prayers and get to class on time. Then he could use the hour after classes and before dinner for homework. After dinner he would read Latin.

John liked his Latin professor. His name was Professor Cordier. He promised the students that if they showed adequate proficiency in translating Latin, he would allow them to study from the Latin Vulgate Bible. The Vulgate was the version of the Bible that had been translated into Latin from Greek by a priest named Jerome about 400 years after the birth of Christ. It had been the official Bible of the Church for nine hundred years. John could hardly wait to read the Bible for himself. What mysteries would it contain? What truths would it reveal? He decided to give extra attention to his Latin studies in order to prove himself worthy.

At the end of class Professor Cordier said something that puzzled John. He said that the first lesson his students must learn was to love their Lord Jesus Christ. John thought that was an odd thing to say. Wasn't everyone in the school seeking religious training? Surely we have already learned that lesson, John thought.

During the midday break John took a walk. It felt good to use his legs after the long morning of lessons. He marvelled at the profusion of houses and people, all in one place. Everywhere he looked there were houses packed one right next to the other. The upper stories hung out over the street, as though the houses squeezed one another so tightly that they had to bulge out overhead. Spires and domes surrounded him. John's father had told him that just last year a man named Magellan had been

30

the first to sail around the entire earth. The city of Paris was so big that John felt as though he had circled the globe himself.

John reached the Seine River which flowed sluggishly through the middle of Paris. He crossed the bridge to the Isle de la Cité. He entered the Cathedral of Notre Dame and made the sign of the cross. The stained glass windows shimmered like jewels on this April day. He lit a candle for his mother, then turned to go.

As he was leaving, he noticed another young man who wore the same cap and gown that he did. From across the cathedral, their eyes met and the stranger quickened his steps to walk alongside John. Once they were outside the holy cathedral, the stranger hailed John.

"Hello," the student said in a cheerful voice, "It looks as though we are going the same way. Do you mind if I join you?"

Immediately John recognized the voice. "Pierre!" he cried. "I did not even recognize you!"

"That's what my mother says, too," Pierre said jokingly. "You must call me Olivétan now. Even my name has changed."

John laughed. "It's good to see you. I was hoping to find you as soon as possible. Tell me everything you have done since I saw you last."

Olivétan began by telling John the things that he should know about the university. He told him how fortunate he was to be able to board with his uncle, since the university housing was more famous for its cockroaches than for its food. "We call the cockroaches our short-winged hawks!" he said.

He told him which professors were good, and which ones were strict. "Watch out for Professor Tempete," he said with emphasis. "They call him the "*Horrida Tempesta*," because he is so severe."

By the time they reached the university, the mid-day break was over and Olivétan still had more to say. He accompanied John to the steps of his college. Before he left he said softly, "John, what you said about not recognizing me was more true than you know. I'm not the same person I was when I started at the university. Knowledge changes things. Beware, it will change you, too."

John pondered Olivétan's words as he entered his classroom. What did he mean by change?

Guadeamus igitur,
Juvenes dum sumus.

(Let us live then and be glad,
While young life is before us.)

~ *Students' song*

5
AD FONTES

John could smell the heat rising off the cobblestones. In his room above his uncle's shop, John tried to ignore the heat by copying some passages from the Latin Bible that Professor Cordier had assigned. He rested his forehead in his hand and concentrated on the book before him.

"Let us live then and be glad . . ." The loud singing of several students floated in through the open window. John paused long enough from his studies to peer out the window. He groaned inwardly. Claude was one of the rowdy students!

Last week Claude received a warning for getting drunk and making a disturbance. John worried that if he got into trouble again, he would be dismissed from the university.

"Claude!" John shouted from his window. The brawlers did not hear him, and continued their boisterous song.

JOHN WARNS CLAUDE AND HIS FRIEND

Across the street another head appeared from a window. An elderly man yelled, "If you boys don't stop your noise-making, I will call the *gendarmes*!"

John pulled on his gown and flew down the steps to the street. The young men carried torches. In the glare of their light, John stopped squarely in front of the drunken group.

"Look, it's the Accusative Case," slurred Claude.

John winced at the nickname. The accusative case was a term for a noun form in Latin. Claude had dubbed him the Accusative Case when John started confronting him about his careless behavior at the university.

34

John knew he had to think quickly. He said, "I came to warn you that a neighbor has threatened to send for the gendarmes. You couldn't hear him shouting at you because of the noise you're making."

At the word, "gendarme," a hush fell on the group, as though each was thinking his own thoughts about the French police and their horrible prison. "Hark to the Accusative Case," Claude called out merrily. "To bed with you all, or we'll be spending the night on the prison floor!"

John thought Claude's lighthearted words hid a trace of fear. The young men quickly dispersed. Only Claude remained. "You won't tell my uncle about this, will you?" he asked.

John put a steadying hand on Claude's shoulder. "Your uncle asked me to look out for you. Claude, we have a serious task here at the university. We must prepare to serve Mother Church."

Claude flashed one of his winning smiles. "I know you'll help me remember that!" Impulsively, he embraced John and quoted the familiar words from their childhood game. "I owe to you both my life and whatever I have!"

John watched Claude dash toward his apartment. He wondered if Claude was really serious about being a priest. He must talk with him sometime when he was sober.

ഇരുജ

With a heavy heart, John crossed the bridge to the Cathedral of Notre Dame. This morning John had an urgent need for prayer. The tension between Claude and himself had grown during the past few weeks. Claude would not listen to John's advice. He claimed that he knew what he was doing. He had only to attend his courses and keep out of trouble at the Sorbonne University, and one day his famous uncle, the Bishop of Noyon, would procure him a nice position in the Church. John doubted that Claude could keep out of trouble.

John climbed the steps to the Cathedral of Notre Dame, the "Cathedral of Our Lady." Surely the Virgin Mary knew great sorrows. John would pour out his heart to her.

John found a quiet chapel and lit some candles. He prayed fervently, calling on every Saint he had ever heard of, and especially petitioning the Virgin Mary. He did not know how long he knelt in prayer, but suddenly he became aware of tolling bells and harsh shouts from outside the cathedral. John quickly ran outside.

The courtyard was filled with an angry mob. John pushed his way to the middle of it. He saw a stake set up. Gendarmes were roughly tying a frail monk to the pole, while the executioner piled wood around his feet. A great torch blazed nearby in readiness.

A figure in a black robe detached itself from the crowd and confronted the prisoner. "Will you recant your Lutheran heresies and submit to Mother Church?" he said in a voice loud enough to be heard by the crowd.

The frail monk straightened and declared, "I die for the true faith that salvation is the gift of God!"

The black figure slapped the prisoner. He motioned to the executioner, who hurried forward to tie a gag on the monk's mouth.

John could not bear to watch. The crowd around him surged forward to see the execution. John shoved with all his strength to get away. As he reached the fringes of the mob, he heard a cracked voice calling out: "This man deserves to die because he will not give up the Lutheran heresy!"

John ran for the bridge back to the Latin Quarter. He dodged the booksellers with their willow baskets of books and pushed through the thickening crowd. Someone called his name. John turned to find the serious face of Olivétan.

"I thought I saw you at Notre Dame," began Olivétan. "I wondered if you would like to talk."

John nodded silently and followed his cousin to a small inn. They sat at a table, and Olivétan began, "You probably expected to find a lot of new things at the university."

John pressed his hands against his forehead. "I never expected anything like this."

"No one ever does," said Olivétan grimly. "John, have you heard the term *ad fontes*?"

"Ad fontes. That means 'back to the sources.'"

"Yes, people like Erasmus want to get back to the sources."

"I remember getting in trouble once with my father for mentioning that name," said John.

Olivétan nodded soberly. "Erasmus is respected as one of the leading humanists, which means he thinks people should use reason to rediscover old truths. There is so much we can learn from the old cultures, but there is a danger, too."

"I don't understand," said John.

"The problem is that several years ago Erasmus published the New Testament in Greek. Suddenly, scholars and priests could read the teachings of Jesus in the original languages."

John interrupted. "I don't see why that is dangerous. Only people who are trained in such things would be handling the Holy Scripture."

Olivétan studied John for a moment as though gauging how much he should say. "John, some of the most learned men in the world have read the Greek text and they have discovered that the Church is teaching falsehood!"

Falsehood! The word hung in the air between John and Pierre like a bared sword. John clutched at his chair to steady himself. A hundred conflicting thoughts coursed through his brain: Martin Luther nailing the ninety-five theses to his church door, Ulrich Zwingli reforming the Church in Switzerland, the stories of executions that were whispered among the students. John did not want to hear anymore.

"I must go now." He stumbled over his chair. The people around him blurred. Somehow he found the door and lost himself in the surging crowd. For hours he walked. His mind was too numb to ask questions.

Volo facere libens quae alius animo faciet.

*(I wish to do willingly what
another man will do in a passion.)*

~ De Clementia, by Seneca

6

THE PHYSICIAN'S SON

John followed the flickering tapers of other students who were arriving at the College of Montaigu. John had graduated from his first year of university study, and had been transferred to this college. He wore the hooded uniform of his new school for the first time.

John found the new college to be similar to the College de la Marche, except for an extra chapel service at four in the morning. Lectures followed at six. Next there was morning Mass before the main class, which took place from eight to ten in the morning. The students discussed the lecture for an hour, then had dinner while the professor read from Scripture. The next hour the students recited lessons and answered questions from a professor. Afternoon class lasted two hours, and then there were prayers, more discussion, and supper before bed at nine in the evening.

John looked for a place to sit. Most of the students still nodded with drowsiness, but John met the eye of one young man who sat alertly at a bench. John sat next to him.

"I'm Nicholas Cop," said the young man.

"I recognize your name," ventured John. "Are you the son of the King's physician?"

"I am. May I ask your name?"

"I'm John Calvin."

"Well, John Calvin, welcome to the College of Montaigu. Am I correct in guessing that you have just finished your first year of being a *summulist*, and are beginning your second year as a logician?"

"How did you know?" asked John in surprise.

"It was simple! You looked as though you did not know where you were going. Also, Professor Cordier is a friend of mine. He told me to look out for you. I'm a physicist. That's what we call the third year students. Let me know if I can help you in any way."

The class began. The professor of theology was Professor Beda. He was the new head of the Faculty of Theology. He was a tall man with large bones. His pinched nose gave him a superior air. When something pleased him he gave a thin bitter smile. He opened the class with several repetitions of material that the students were to memorize. John concentrated fiercely to catch up with the rest of the class.

Next the professor divided the class into small groups for debate. The professor paired John with Nicholas Cop. Nicholas opened the debate with a carefully reasoned statement which he supported with writings from Augustine, who was one of the Church fathers. John, who had to argue the opposite point, responded with several quotes from Aristotle.

Nicholas looked surprised. Aristotle's *Logic* and *Physics* were not taught until the second and third year at the university. He parried John's response with a Greek quote of the New Testament, which he then translated into Latin.

It was John's turn to look surprised. Few people could read the New Testament in Greek. He was about to ask Nicholas how he knew the quote in Greek, when a look from his debate partner warned him to keep silent. By looking out of the corner of his eye, John could see that Professor Beda was standing at his shoulder. His narrow eyes studied John and Nicholas. John quickly quoted from the *Summulai Logicales*, which was his first year text book on logic. He pointed out the fallacy in Nicholas' argument.

Professor Beda walked to the next group.

Nicholas let out a sigh. "We were getting into waters that were a little too deep for us," he explained in an undertone.

"But how did you know a quote in Greek?" whispered John.

"It's a long story. Can you come to my house for

JOHN HAS A MEAL AT THE COP HOME

dinner this Friday? I will explain it then." John
promised to come, and the two students continued
their debate.

John arrived at the imposing front door of the
Cop home at precisely half past seven, the time that
Nicholas had given him. A uniformed servant
answered the door and ushered him into the sitting

room. Nicholas and his three brothers stood near an ornate fireplace. Nicholas introduced them to John, who liked them immediately. They had open, honest faces like Nicholas.

The doorbell sounded and another guest entered the room. Nicholas welcomed him warmly. "Clement Marot, I would like you to meet my new friend, John Calvin."

Clement Marot was a cheerful man, a few years older than John. He greeted John enthusiastically. Noting the student's robe, he said:

One should consider it an honor,
When Providence brings thee to a scholar.

Nicholas laughed. "You must not take Clement seriously," he said. "He is a valet to the King's sister, Princess Margaret. She likes him because he is always creating verses and poems. Some of them have even been set to music and are quite popular at court."

Nicholas' father entered the room. John judged him to be a little older than his own father. He had twinkling blue eyes and silvery hair. John felt at a loss for words being in the presence of a man who was doctor to kings, but Dr. Cop quickly put him at ease by asking John about his studies.

John and the Cop brothers enjoyed discussing various areas of learning. Nicholas wanted to be a physician like his father. He talked about his lessons on the physical world. At one point in the discussion he turned to his father. "Is it true, Father, that the corpse of someone who has been murdered will bleed afresh in the presence of the murderer?"

The physician looked thoughtful. "I have always heard it is the test for guilt, but I have never seen the test performed."

A debate ensued as to whether it was true. Someone claimed that it must be true since the best sources available said it was true. John ventured to say that an appeal to popular beliefs was not proof.

Nicholas supported John. He posed the question that if it were true, why was the test never used in the Bible.

One of his younger brothers rolled his eyes. "Can you claim to have read every word in the Bible?"

"Yes," replied Nicholas.

Nicholas's brother began a new debate as to whether the Bible contained every form of justice known to man. John listened and thought about the debate he had with Nicholas in class. How did he know so much about the Bible?

Dr. Cop led his guests to the dining room. A pewter plate, mug, and silver knife gleamed at each place. A man in a blue uniform served roast lamb and *chou rouge à la flamande*. John had never heard of the second dish. It proved to be red cabbage cut into strips and cooked in a casserole with butter, diced pippins, onions, and red wine.

After long hours of study and simple foods, John enjoyed the dinner. He felt warmed by both the food and the conversation.

Nicholas walked with John back to his uncle's home.

"I promised to tell you how I knew the Bible quote in Greek," began Nicholas.

"I guess I was surprised that you knew it," began John. "The only person I know who can quote Greek is Olivétan."

Nicholas gave John a piercing glance. "You know Olivétan?" he asked.

"He's my cousin."

Nicholas lapsed into silence. John had the feeling that he was being measured for some reason.

Nicholas began hesitantly, "There are several of us who are studying the Bible in the original languages. That is how I know Professor Cordier so well. He says that we should invite you to join us, but I wanted to get to know you better first. After talking with you tonight I agree with the professor."

John felt honored to receive the invitation, but something in Nicholas' manner made him wary.

"This is a serious invitation, John," Nicholas continued. "You must never reveal who is in this group."

"Are you saying the university does not approve of this group?" asked John.

"No," said Nicholas firmly. "These are dangerous

times. I trust you, John. Will you come?"

"I will have to think about it," John said cautiously. A growing uneasiness replaced the contented feeling John had felt after the delightful meal. A dangerous decision lay before him. It could change his life forever. Was he willing to take the risk for the sake of more knowledge?

Nicholas whispered quickly, "If you decide to come, meet at the House of the Pelican on Rue St. Martin. The proprietor is Monsieur de la Forge. Tell him that you are there for the study and he will show you where to go." Nicholas walked swiftly back the way he had come. John watched him disappear down the cobbled road. The first words he had learned in Latin came back to him: *Magnae et longae viae.* Great and long roads. What was the road that Nicholas wanted him to walk?

As pants the hart for streams of living water,
So longeth my soul for Thee, O God.

~Psalm translated and set to music
by Clement Marot

7

THE HOUSE
OF THE PELICAN

At the House of the Pelican, beef browned on a spit above a huge hearth. Dozens of students crowded around the tables. John pressed himself into the corner bench and tried to look inconspicuous. He nonchalantly studied the bow window and heavy lamps hanging from the beamed ceiling.

"What can I get for you, sir?" asked a burly man wearing a spattered apron.

"I'm here for a study," John said hoarsely. His mouth felt so dry that he could barely form the words.

The man motioned for him to follow. John wedged himself through the mass of jovial students drinking wine in mugs. John realized with relief that no one seemed to notice him.

"I am Etienne de la Forge," the man said quietly, as he led John to a back stairway. "Knock three times

47

on the door at the top of the stairs, and you will find the study."

"Thank you." John took the stairs two at a time and rapped three times on the door before he could lose his courage.

The door quickly opened and a hand pulled him into the room. The next moment he found himself face to face with his cousin.

"Olivétan!" he cried. "I did not expect to find you here."

"Nor I you," said Olivétan as he embraced his cousin heartily.

Nicholas Cop stepped forward. "John, I hoped you would come."

"We are translating the Bible into French," explained Olivétan. He introduced John to several other men who wore the robes of students. He directed John to sit on one of the benches. "John, you may look on with me. I will read what we have written."

Olivétan began to read. His deep voice grew softer as he read. John thought with surprise, he really loves the Bible.

Olivétan read:

This then is the message which we have heard of him, and declare unto you, that God is light, and in him is no darkness at all. If we say that we have fellowship with him, and walk in darkness, we lie, and do not the truth; But if we walk in the light, as he is in the light, we have fellowship one with another, and the blood of Jesus Christ his Son cleanses us from all sin.

Olivétan strung the French words together like

pearls on a string. John was accustomed to hearing the Bible intoned in Latin in the hollow voice of a priest. But these verses were different. What did it mean, "The blood of Jesus Christ his Son cleanses us from all sin?" John forgot to follow the rest of the reading as he pondered this question.

John met regularly with the men who were translating the Bible during the next year. The circle of Bible students gradually widened. A lame cobbler named Milon came. He thirsted for the Scriptures in his own language. Clement Marot came to listen as the scholars worked. He began to write hymns for Princess Margaret. Etienne de la Forge, who provided the secret room for the meeting, came when he could. He had come to believe in God through the writings of Luther. He paid to have portions of the French scriptures printed. Monsieur de la Forge sheltered Flemish refugees who were persecuted for their faith. They also attended the meetings.

John completed the requirement to be a third year physicist in record time. He was in his last year of the *trivium*.

It was the year 1525, and Paris was the center of a gathering storm. While the courtiers sang the popular hymns of Clement Marot, the university faculty de-nounced the new "enlightenment" that was taking place.

Pope Adrian VI supported the faculty. He resolved to root out any heresy against Mother Church. When a rumor circulated that someone was preparing a Bible translation in French for the common people, Rector Beda angrily denounced the idea. He cast a suspicious eye toward Olivétan.

John walked swiftly down the side street to a

small door. The night came early these days. He glanced behind him but could not see anyone in the lowering dusk. He knocked quietly on the narrow wooden door. The door swung inward and John stepped through.

A single candle glowed in the middle of the room. A tall thin man with a Flemish accent spoke softly to the group. "Brethren, we must remain true to God, even in the face of persecution. The Bible calls those blessed who persevered to the end.

"Many of you have heard of Professor LeFevre. We use the Hebrew Old Testament that he prepared many years ago. We have just received word that Professor Lefevre's writings are banned by the Sorbonne University. The translations of the New Testament that he made and his writings about the true Gospel were burned. We do not know what will happen next. We must look to God for strength and guidance."

John joined the circle of men and women around the single candle. The tall man prayed for the believers in the city of Paris.

The next week, the smoke from a fire rose above the city of Paris. John could not look at it. An Augustinian monk had been burned for succumbing to the Lutheran heresy. John knew people who believed as the monk did. What would happen to them? What would happen to their children?

John heard footsteps on the backstairs. Olivétan slipped into the room. He wore his travelling cloak.

"John, I came to say good-bye."

John breathed the bitter smell of smoke. "You are leaving?"

"They are burning any pieces of the Bible that

they can find."

"And your copy of the translation?"

Olivétan pointed to the lining of his coat. "It is safe as long as I am."

"Where will you go?" asked John.

"I do not know yet. They say that Princess Margaret protects many believers in Angouleme. I will communicate with you somehow."

"What will happen to the meetings?"

Olivétan's eyes flashed. "You must not go to them for a while. It is too dangerous."

John feared for his cousin's safety. Why couldn't Olivétan remain content with Mother Church? Was it possible to be content with the Church as it was now? John wanted to try.

ഇൽ ൽ

On the bridge of Avignon,
People dance, People dance,
On the bridge of Avignon,
People dance all around.

The children held hands and sang the folk song.

Nicholas Cop kept his eyes on the children while he quietly narrated the news he had heard to John. "The Bishop of Meaux was teaching the true Gospel to his people. So many people believed on Christ that he had to send for preachers to help teach the people.

"One young preacher became famous for his fiery passion. He has red hair to match. His name is William Farel, and I will guess that this is not the last you will hear of him."

51

The children began a new game with a ball. They begged John to play with them.

"Not today, little ones. I will watch from here."

When the children were safely out of hearing, Nicholas continued. "Things are not right since King Francis was captured."

John nodded thoughtfully. He remembered his first day in Paris and the proud palace of King Francis which was called the *Louvre*. Its grand dimensions matched the ambitions of this proud king who was constantly battling for more land.

Nicholas interrupted his thoughts. "The parliament has grown bold since King Francis was put in prison in Madrid. They called the Bishop of Meaux before them several times and warned him to stop teaching the Gospel to the people."

John shifted uncomfortably. It was one thing when a professor was banned because of his faith, but a Bishop! The Bishops were the pillars of the Church. Could they be stopped from teaching the Bible?

"What did the Bishop do?" asked John.

"He didn't listen at first, but then they threatened to remove him from his position. He promised that he would not teach the Lutheran heresies. The preachers of Meaux had to flee."

"What happened to the people?"

"They showed more faithfulness than their Bishop." Nicholas lowered his voice. "Many were burned at the stake."

John felt a wrenching pain in his stomach. He could not bear the news of more executions.

God is always near his chosen ones;
for although they sometimes turn their backs
upon him, he nevertheless has always
his fatherly eye turned towards us.

~ John Calvin

8

A NEW ROAD

On a chilly September day, John journeyed home to receive a new benefice. It was the pastorate of Saint-Martin-de-Martheville, a little village near Noyon.

John was in his *quadrivium*, or fourth, year of school. He was studying arithmetic, geometry, astronomy, and music. He would conclude with a master's exam. If he passed, he would receive the master of arts degree and could study theology, law, or medicine.

John arrived at the outskirts of the village. He led his horse through the back alleys where garbage rotted in the streets. He thought of Nicholas, who was studying medicine now. He told John that some doctors thought sickness spread faster where there was a lot of filth. He told John, "There is a law in the city of London that you must cart away your rubbish and not throw it in the streets. The city council fines people who do not keep the street in front of their homes clean. They think it will improve health."

John directed his horse to the church. His father and brother, Antoine, were already there. Antoine had grown since John last saw him. He was fourteen now. He swept off his hat and showed John his tonsured head.

"What do you think of my hair cut?" he asked impishly. "I just received your old benefice. I will be a priest like my brothers."

John's father had aged greatly since he had seen him last. His shoulders sagged as with a great load. His face was pale.

John pulled Antoine aside. "Why does Papa look so tired?"

"You must not talk about it," whispered Antoine. "Charles says it is very serious. There is trouble with the cathedral chapter of Noyon over a business matter. We hope it will soon be settled."

Unfortunately, Papa could not settle the matter. While John studied in Paris, his father's troubles had increased. At nineteen, John became one of the youngest scholars to finish the required courses. Before he could begin his studies for the priesthood, he received an urgent summons from his father.

John found his father in bed. Charles nervously paced the floor of his room. "How long has he been like this?" asked John.

"Since the last meeting with the canons. Mother

says there was a terrible argument. You know how stubborn Papa is. One of the canons wanted him to cheat on the settlement of an inheritance, and Papa refused to do it. They threatened to excommunicate him."

"What did Papa do?"

"He threw them out of the house. He was so upset that he got a fever during the night. He has not been himself."

"John." It was Papa's voice.

John and Charles hurried to their father's side. Papa gripped John's arm and raised himself to a sitting position.

"I have made a decision," he said. His voice was weak but his eyes glinted with his usual determination. "John, you must not study to be a priest. I am sending you to study law."

John gasped. "Papa, do you know what you are saying?"

Papa closed his eyes and leaned back against his pillow. "I have made my decision."

Charles pulled John from the room. "You must do what Papa says," he said bleakly. "He has his reasons."

₨₳₩

The leaves on the trees blazed gold and orange the day John arrived in Orleans to study law. He saw stone buildings rising above a sparkling river. Near

JOHN WRITES A LESSON FOR THEODORE

the school of law, enthusiastic students played a fashionable new game called tennis.

John found a boarding house on a quiet street near the school. Though his father's sudden decision perplexed him, he anticipated satisfying hours of quiet study in this new town.

The first day at the law school, John met Professor Wolmar. He taught Greek. He learned that John had been studying the language.

"What does a lawyer need with Greek?" he asked John.

"I was studying the Bible," replied John quietly.

The professor raised his eyebrows. "Indeed? Then there is someone that you need to meet."

The next day Professor Wolmar knocked on the worm-eaten door of a small boarding house. Before he could introduce John to the person who answered the door, John cried, "Olivétan!"

The cousins sat at Olivétan's table and caught up on the news of the past year, while the professor sat in bewildered silence.

"How is my family?" asked Olivétan. "I could not go home or let anyone know where I was."

"Your mother is well. And how is the translation?"

"I was able to escape with the full Hebrew text that Professor Lefevre had prepared. I have finished the Old Testament and hope to finish the New Testament soon. Professor Wolmar is helping me with that since he is a Greek scholar."

John met regularly with Olivétan and Professor Wolmar to translate the Bible. He also applied himself to his law studies. John reviewed what he learned every evening before he went to sleep. When he awoke, he reviewed the material again. He committed vast amounts of his law studies to memory. John's teachers recognized his abilities and asked him to teach some of the classes.

A year later, Orleans became too dangerous for

the Bible translation work. Olivétan travelled to the German city state of Strasbourg. John's father sent him to Bourges to study under the famous lawyer, Alciat. Professor Wolmar also moved to Bourges, because Princess Margaret extended religious protection there.

In Professor Wolmar's home, John met a boy named Theodore de Beza. Theodore was twelve. Professor Wolmar tutored the boy in Greek.

One day Professor Wolmar asked John to teach Theodore since he could not be there. John took his task seriously. As he considered what to teach Theodore, he thought of Professor Cordier who had been his first and best teacher. What was the first lesson he had given the students? John remembered. He wrote in Greek for Theodore: "The first lesson you must learn is to love Jesus Christ."

The certainty which rests on God's Word exceeds all knowledge.

~John Calvin

9

A SUDDEN CONVERSION

Antoine and Charles greeted John as he tied his horse to the post. Antoine's eyes looked larger than ever in his pale face. Charles looked as though he had been crying.

"Papa will not recover," Charles said quietly. "I knew you would want to come."

With a heavy heart, John mounted the stairs to his father's room. He found his father sleeping on his bed. John knelt and began to pray. The room grew dark. Charles and Antoine joined John.

In the early morning hours Papa awoke. He was too weak to talk, but he recognized John and clasped his hand. Charles administered the last rites for him. Surrounded by his family, Gerard Calvin died.

Charles offered to make the arrangements for the burial. He returned midmorning in a hot rage.

"John, they are denying Papa a Christian burial!"

"How can they do that?" asked John.

"They say that he was excommunicated before he died. It was that senseless controversy with the canons."

John was thoughtful. "Could you tell me the details? I may be able to challenge their decision."

Charles pulled out some papers and carefully described the history of the problem. John formulated a plan to defend his father against his accusers. He made an appointment with the canons.

"I will go all the way to the Bishop if I have to," he told Charles and Antoine.

The canons were impressed with the learning and achievements of the young man who appeared before them. They listened to his well-reasoned arguments and they softened. After a short consultation, they told John that he might bury his father in holy ground and have a Mass said for him.

John remained in Noyon for a month. He lived once again in his childhood home on the Wheat Market Square. Antoine had grown into a young scholar. Marie was a vivacious little girl. Mama had taught her to cook. She proudly served John the stew she made by herself. They made a cheerful household with Antoine and Marie's youthful chatter. Only Charles remained silent.

One evening Charles stopped for a visit. John noticed deep furrows in Charles' careworn face.

"Tell me what has been happening in Noyon,"

he urged Charles.

"It is changing just like the rest of the world," Charles said with a sigh.

John remembered the heated talks that Charles used to have with Papa. Charles was the one who wanted things to change.

"What do you mean by change?"asked John.

Charles smiled for the first time since Papa's death. At last he broke the painful silence. He told John of the schemings and corruption of the churchmen of Noyon. He told of the dangers of opposing such men. "But there are still some independent-minded men," said Charles. "Do you remember that Bishop de Hangest refused to shave his beard?"

John nodded.

Charles looked around to make sure that no one was listening. "Well, the canons decided that he could not be allowed to break their silly rule, so they locked him out of the cathedral!"

John grinned. "And you were siding with the Bishop?"

"Of course! It is time for people to think for themselves."

"Charles, I agree with you, but I have seen a lot of sadness come to those who thought for themselves. In Paris people have been burned at the stake for their beliefs."

Charles eyes blazed. "And I would burn with them."

"I could not," John said quietly. "I will stand with you to oppose corruption, but I could never be a heretic. My mind has been so trained to the rites and rules of the Church of Rome that I cannot leave it easily."

Tears sprang to Charles' eyes. He began to speak, and then stopped himself. "John," he said at last, "Now that Papa is dead it is even more important that you think for yourself."

When Charles left, John sat quietly in the dark room. Charles spoke the truth more than he could ever know. Papa had been the guide of John's young life. He must learn to make his own decisions now.

The first decision that John made was to return to Paris. He wanted to be a scholar rather than a lawyer. He arranged for rooms in the Latin Quarter, where he could study and write.

The apartment was on the third floor of a house that let out onto a small courtyard. John could look out of his window and see the children playing in the small area.

John wrote a commentary on an essay by Seneca, who was a Roman statesman and philosopher. It was exciting to be one of the men to lead others back to the literature of the Greeks and Romans. John wrote his commentary in eight short months. He proudly took it to the printer. On a fine April morning John held the first copy in his hands.

He dedicated the book to his old friend, Claude de Hangest, who was now the abbot of Saint Eloi's monastery in Noyon. John wrote in the preface:

Accept this, the first of my fruits. It belongs of right to you, for I owe to you both myself and whatever I have, and especially, because I was brought up as a child in your house.

Despite the accomplishment of publishing his first book, John felt restless. His greatest desire was to attain the station of scholar and be able to devote himself to writing. The closer he came to his goal, however, the less peace he felt.

John returned to Orleans for a few months to finish his law studies. The faculty unanimously awarded a doctorate of law to him.

Next he visited Noyon. John and Charles had lively debates about the teachings of the Bible. Charles sounded like Professor Wolmar and Olivétan when he spoke of the "Gospel of Christ." He told John flatly, "Saying the prayers in your rosary and knowing a lot about the Bible does not make you a child of God." A familiar pang clutched John's stomach. Charles was a Lutheran!

John threw himself into studying the Bible and some of the Church fathers such as Augustine. He must help Charles before it was too late. As he studied, however, a very different doctrine presented itself to his mind. John tried to resist the new ideas. They contradicted everything he had been taught. John, however, realized that he must face the new ideas honestly, and he knew what he had to do. He returned to Paris.

The wooden sign of the House of the Pelican banged in the breeze. John paused before he entered. He hoped that he was doing the right thing.

Etienne de la Forge smiled broadly when he saw John. He led him swiftly up the familiar back stairs. There were many new faces in the room, but John recognized the lame cobbler, Milon. A Bible reading was in progress. John sat at the back of the room and listened.

A man read a long passage from the book of Ephesians. John recognized passages that he had studied with Olivétan. Copies of their translations must have survived. Some of the people silently mouthed the words. They had heard the Bible passage so frequently that they had memorized it.

As John listened intently, he felt his old stubbornness melting away. It was a frightening feeling.

John rushed home after the meeting and immersed himself in reading his Bible. With every line that he read, the simple truths of the faith grew clearer in his mind. He realized that these new ideas were actually older than his long-cherished beliefs. His study of the Bible was leading him back to the source of true faith. Passages that he had committed to memory long ago were full of new meaning.

*Evangelion (Gospel) means,
"The glad and delightful message of grace
exhibited to us in Christ."*

~ John Calvin

10

SHOES OF FAITH

John caught his reflection in the thick glass window of a shop. He saw a long thin face and serious eyes. The black scholar's gown made him look older than his twenty-four years.

"Who am I now?" John asked his reflection. He would be happy to call himself a scholar and live in a quiet corner of Paris where he could study and write. His life, however, had been anything but quiet lately.

There was the meeting at the House of the Pelican when he told Nicholas and Etienne de la Forge about his new faith. Nicholas walked home with him. The two old friends talked until dawn about the faith that was clearly described in the Bible.

John confided to Nicholas. "It was hard for me to admit that I had all my life been in ignorance and error. It was as if a light broke in upon me. I suddenly saw in what a dunghill of error I had wallowed. I trembled at the prospect of eternal death. I could do no other than to take myself to God's way at once."

The next day a flustered monk in a gray cowl appeared at John's door.

"I was told I might learn of God's plan of salvation here," he told John.

John ushered him into his room before the other boarders could hear any more.

"Sir," the monk said, "I came to you because I heard that you were a man who has taken vows to Mother Church, as I have. I am hoping you will understand my confusions. Until last week I was certain that if I did my religious duties and served penance in Purgatory, I would go to Heaven at the last."

"What happened to change your mind?"

"I came across a little booklet that contained a chapter of the Bible translated into French. I read that, 'All have sinned and fallen short of the glory of God.' At first I was angry to read it. Then I thought of sins that I have committed, and I felt miserable."

John took a piece of parchment from his desk. "I understand your misery, but it is truly a blessing to you. The Bible teaches us that we are sinners. Those who do not yet understand this are like people who are asleep. God is waking you up!"

"But I still do not understand."

"Look at this scripture that I have copied into French. It is from the Gospel of John. Gospel means 'the glad and delightful message of grace exhibited to us in Christ.' If you will read this, I think you will understand."

Hungrily the man took the paper and began to read aloud, "In the beginning was the Word, and the Word was with God, and the Word was God."

He read the entire passage. He ended with, "But as many as received him, to them gave he power to become the sons of God, even to them that believe on his name."

John explained that the Word was Jesus. "Jesus not only was God, but he became man so that he could die for our sins. When we believe on His name, we become 'sons of God,'" John said.

"But what of the rules that I have kept so closely all my life? I have never missed a Mass. I say my prayers everyday. I have tried to be good . . ."

John pointed again to the Bible passage. "Here it says, 'The law was given by Moses, but grace and truth came by Jesus Christ.' We cannot be good enough to satisfy the law of Moses. That is why Jesus came. He makes us sons of God as a gift."

The man clutched the parchment. John could see in his face that he was struggling with these new ideas.

"May I pray for you?" John asked.

"Yes."

John began: "Lord, we pray that we may surrender ourselves altogether to You. Please enable us to understand and obey your Word alone, so that we may not deviate either to the right hand or to the left. Help us to understand that You alone are wise. Help us to acknowledge our sin and vanity. Teach us by your holy Word. In the name of Jesus Christ, Amen."

Tears streamed down the face of the monk. "I never heard a prayer in French before," he said hoarsely. "All my life I have only prayed in words that I memorized. I did not know that you could talk to God like that."

The next week the monk visited John again. "I have been talking to God all week," he announced, "And the Lord has been gracious to me!" He held out the parchment from the Gospel of John, but John insisted that he keep it.

"Perhaps you can share it with someone else," John said with a chuckle. "God seems to have this special task for those who have taken vows to serve Him!"

The next day a young student had questions for John. Later, a rich merchant named Du Bourg drew John aside for a quiet conference. A man from Picardy sought out John, too. A steady stream of visitors mounted the steps to John's small room. His private study had become as busy as a school. John found that he relished the opportunity to talk about the Savior who made people into sons of God.

A thunderstorm rumbled in the summer heat as the people gathered to hear the Bible read. The room brimmed with men and women who wedged themselves into every available spot. John sat quietly between a husky leather worker and his old friend, the lame cobbler, Milon. Milon's cane poked John in the ribs.

Nicholas Cop read the Bible. John heard the man next to him weeping as Nicholas read, "Therefore, if any man be in Christ, he is a new creature: old things are passed away." John thought of the young student who had met with him that day. He had rejoiced to hear the truth about Jesus. How hungry people were for the words of the Bible!

Nicholas finished and caught John's eye. "We are blessed to have a Bible scholar in our midst this evening. His name is John Calvin. He will tell you that he is new to the faith, but his understanding of the Holy Bible is great. I would like him to speak a few words of encouragement to you."

John rose hesitantly and made his way to the front of the room. He looked at the faces of the people. Several of them were old friends and they smiled their encouragement.

"As you know, many of us were hopelessly lost in superstitions, but God in His great mercy has shown us the true way. As Jesus said, 'I am the way, the truth, and the life: No man cometh unto the Father but by me.'"

The verses that John had labored to study during his years as a student came easily to his mind. He fluently translated them into French. One verse followed another. Many of the passages were not yet available in French for these people. They sighed in contentment as John recited long sections.

Milon, the lame cobbler, remained after the meeting. "Tell me that passage from the book of Romans again," he asked John. "We lost that book of the Bible when Olivétan had to flee with the manuscript."

John sat next to the gentle man and quoted every passage of Romans that he had memorized. "Next time I will bring my Latin Bible and read it all to you," he promised.

That night John could not sleep. In his mind he saw the humble cobbler. He could not walk, but he spent his life making shoes for those who could. John thought of the past few years when he could not believe, but had made Bible translations for those who could. How little his studies had benefited him until God had brought him to faith! But now he could walk in his own faith. John had a lot of work to do.

ℬℭℛ

The children in the courtyard sang:

Are you sleeping,
Are you sleeping,
Brother John, Brother John?
Morning bells are ringing,
Morning bells are ringing,
Din, Don, Din,
Din, Don, Din.

John sat on the front steps with Etienne de la Forge's infant son on his knee. A little girl with blonde braids broke away from the crowd of children and pointed to John. "Let's ask him!" she cried.

The band of children ran to John. "Monsieur John, are you really Brother John?" they asked.

John laughed. "Why do you ask?"

A boy with bristly brown hair said, "We know you are because you don't have any hair on top of your head."

John remembered the time the children snatched his hat during a game. Several eyes had opened wide when they saw his tonsure.

John answered, "My hair is cut this way because I took a vow to serve Mother Church, but I am not a monk like Brother John."

The children looked disappointed. The bristly-haired boy said, "My Papa said that you went to see Princess Margaret."

The children clamored to hear more. "Did you see the Italian girl that married Prince Henry?"

The girl with blonde braids said, "My Mama says her name is Catherine de Medici and she has taught everyone the Italian *balleto*."

"Did you see the balleto?" a dozen voices asked.

John held his finger to his lips and pointed to the sleeping baby on his lap. The children huddled close to John on the steps and waited for him to tell his story.

"It is true that I went to the palace of King Francis. It is called the Louvre. It is a huge drafty place with more furniture than in all your houses put together. The furniture is all covered with blue and gold brocade and there are tapestries on the walls."

The children's eyes grew wide as they imagined the splendor of the palace.

John continued. "There are children a little older than you who are pages in the palace. They have to stand at attention. Princess Margaret, who is the King's sister, asked me to visit her at the Louvre."

"Was she pretty?"

"Of course, but the most beautiful thing about Princess Margaret is that she loves God."

The children thought about this for a moment. Then one of the older boys said, "Let's pretend that we are pages and we have to stand at attention!"

The children scattered to play their new game.

John sat holding the baby and remembering his visit with Princess Margaret. She was a sincere Christian. When John defended a book about faith that the princess had written, she invited him to the palace. She promised to do what she could to encourage true Christianity in France.

The princess also encouraged John to write a book. "The new Christians need the Gospel presented in a simple way," she told him.

Nearly the whole of sacred doctrine
consists in these two parts:
knowledge of God and of ourselves.

~ John Calvin

11
A HOPE FOR THE CHURCH

John sat pensively at his desk. His forehead rested in his hand as he studied the Bible before him. He was trying to grasp the best way to explain the truths of the Gospel.

At the top of a fresh piece of paper John wrote the headings, "Knowledge of God," and "Knowledge of Man."

In the Bible people could learn the truth about God. They could also learn about themselves. John realized that everyone he had met, from cobblers to princesses, thirsted for this knowledge: the truth about God and themselves. That was the delight of the Bible! One could learn so much. Next, John wrote a heading called "The Law." He would explain about sin there. Next he wrote, "God's Love in Christ."

Carefully, John presented the Gospel as though he were laying forth a case in the courtroom. He must base every point on fact.

John prayed fervently as he wrote. If only God would work in the hearts of the leaders of the Church, perhaps they could lead Mother Church back to the Bible.

John heard a baritone voice singing with the children in the courtyard. He looked out of the window in time to see Nicholas Cop stride through the middle of a game of Avignon Bridge. John ran down the stairs to meet his friend.

"You are looking at the new rector of the four faculties of the university," Nicholas announced.

John congratulated his friend. "When will you be inaugurated?"

"There will be a ceremony in two weeks. I need your help to write a speech."

John absently wiped the ink from his hands. "Nicholas, you have an unusual opportunity here. Would you consider giving your speech in French?"

Nicholas laughed. "For what purpose? Most speeches are as dry as dust."

"What if this one wasn't?"

Nicholas looked doubtful, but John's eyes sparkled with enthusiasm. "Think of the influence the true Gospel could have if the faculty of the Sorbonne heard it!"

Nicholas and John spent the chilly November evenings writing a speech that was unlike any that the Sorbonne faculty had ever heard. John prayed with every fiber of his being for reform to sweep his church.

At the inauguration ceremony the professors and priests in their ceremonial robes sat stiffly on the wooden benches. They were thinking about the banquet they would have after the necessary speeches were given.

The first man stood and gave a long oration in Latin. The sheen of his velvet robe glowed beautifully in the candlelight. Some of the audience fell asleep.

Nicholas rose to speak next. He wore a red wool gown trimmed with black velvet and the flat cap of a doctor. He greeted the assembly. Heads jerked up. Several professors gasped. He spoke in French!

"Blessed are the poor in spirit." In flawless French prose, the new rector explained the faith of the Bible. He urged his audience to stop the persecutions of those who believed in the Bible. John noticed several monks scurry out of side doors before the speech was finished. Rector Beda sat grim-faced on his bench.

A month later the French parliament summoned Nicholas Cop to appear before them. Two men in uniform appeared at his door to escort him. Nicholas wore the robe of his new office. He walked in dignified silence between the two men.

Suddenly a merry group of students crowded into the narrow street. They were singing a song by Clement Marot. They squeezed between the men in uniform and Nicholas. One student hastily whispered, "Flee for your life. Princess Margaret sends word that Parliament will put you in prison."

Nicholas stepped into a side alley. He quickly removed his robes and mingled with the group of students as they disappeared down another street. The escorts looked at one another in bewilderment. Their charge had disappeared.

Meanwhile, a troop of gendarmes marched toward the boarding house where John lodged. A few of the students wound through back streets in the Latin quarter and arrived moments before the gendarmes.

They raced up the three flights of stairs to John's room.

"You must escape at once!" they told John.

As he grabbed a few papers they tore his sheet into strips and fashioned a rope. They could hear the loud voices of the gendarmes below. John climbed through the window and let himself down into the courtyard. He raced for the safety of the streets where he could melt into the crowds.

The students hid the rope and pretended to be hard at their studies when the gendarmes burst in moments later. They stalled for time as the gendarmes questioned them about John Calvin.

The gendarmes waited, but John Calvin never returned to his apartment. If they had set a guard at the gate of the city, they might have seen a peasant vine dresser, returning to his fields. His smock bulged at one side where some papers were hidden.

ဆ၄၁၃

In time, John made his way on foot to the home of Louis du Tillet. Louis had studied in Paris with John and now served as a canon in the cathedral in Angouleme. He owned a large estate and possessed an excellent library. He secretly supported the Christians in France.

John spent happy days in his friend's library. He called himself Charles d'Espeville, which means, "Charles of the City of Hope." John was an outcast, but he considered that his citizenship was in Heaven, the city of hope.

John devoted himself to writing while he stayed with du Tillet. He felt an urgency to finish the simple explanation of Christianity that he was writing.

John wrote to a friend in Orleans:

I have learned from experience that we cannot see very far before us. When I promised myself an easy, tranquil life, then what I least expected was at hand: and, on the contrary, when it appeared to me that my situation might not be an agreeable one, a quiet nest was built for me, beyond my expectation, and this is the doing of the Lord, to whom, when we commit ourselves, Himself will have a care for us.

John met in a cave near the river with the secret Christians. The people that he met were so hungry for the true Scriptures that John felt a new urgency to write about the Bible. He preached to them: "If God be for us, who can be against us." He taught them that God saves people by grace and not because of the good things that they do.

In every place, crowds gathered to hear the Gospel.

John also travelled to remote areas to preach. Secret believers met in such numbers that John needed a platform to be heard. A Christian carpenter made John a moveable pulpit. He took it with him wherever he preached. The people called themselves "the congregation of the wilderness." The sheer rocks of the mountains were their cathedral walls, and the sky spangled with stars was their vaulted dome.

ഓ⚮൪

The forest trees grew straight and tall. John followed a dirt path that wound through the forest. Presently John reached a simple cottage. He knocked at the door.

An elderly woman opened the door and peered cautiously at John.

"Good day," he began. "I have come to visit Professor Lefevre. Could you tell him that John Calvin is here?"

The woman silently closed the door. She returned a few minutes later and directed him to the single room that opened off the main entrance.

Professor Lefevre was almost one hundred years old. Though his body was frail, his eyes sparkled. "I have heard a few things about you," he told John in greeting.

"I hope I am not intruding," began John. "I need your counsel."

Professor Lefevre lifted bushy eyebrows in astonishment. "What can an old man say that will change anything?"

"You have already made great changes," said John. "Olivétan is even now completing the translation of the Bible that you started."

The professor leaned back in his chair and closed his eyes. John feared that the interview was over. Professor Lefevre said softly, "I never thought I would live to see this day, yet I mourn for my country because I fear the Scriptures will find much opposition in France."

"Do you mean from the King?"

Professor Lefevre sat forward in his chair. "Not only King Francis, but everyone who is under the authority of the Pope. The church leaders and the French Parliament will burn the French Bibles."

"But if there are a lot of sincere believers in the Church, like the ministers in Meaux, don't you think that we could change the Church?"

Professor Lefevre shook his head sadly. "It is too late for that. You, who are young, must teach the true Gospel in a new Church."

John sat stunned for a few minutes. Professor Lefevre had lived his entire life in the Church. How could he give this advice? The old man laid his hand lightly on John's shoulder. "John, I predict that you will be an instrument in restoring the Kingdom of Heaven in France."

John rode from the professor's cottage to his hometown of Noyon. He could no longer hope to enter the priesthood. He resigned his two benefices. They were his last link to the Mother Church that had raised him from childhood.

*Let us . . . become submissive to God,
and then he will convey to us by his Word
nothing but sweetness, nothing but delights.*

~ John Calvin

12

TO HIS MOST CHRISTIAN MAJESTY

The small group of men and women who studied the Bible at the House of the Pelican became a church. The Bible taught them that Jesus Christ died once for sins. They realized that they could not participate in the Mass in the Catholic Church, because the Church taught that in the Mass Jesus was sacrificed every time the bread and wine were given. Though they could be killed for their beliefs, they firmly kept to the Bible teaching that the Lord's Supper was meant as a spiritual communion.

The believers met secretly in various homes. They used passwords and signals to communicate danger. John visited the small congregation. He used his disguise as Charles d'Espeville, so that he would not be imprisoned.

One evening Etienne de la Forge asked John to

speak to the little church. Etienne removed a Latin Bible from a hiding place in the wall. He reverently placed it on a table before John. John opened the book and translated as he read aloud.

Suddenly an owl hooted near the window. It was the signal of danger. "The gendarmes are coming this way!" cried Madame de la Forge.

The men and women left quickly through a back door. John carefully returned the Bible to its hiding place.

Etienne whispered to John, "It is too dangerous for you to remain in Paris. You must move on."

The tramp of heavy feet sounded in the hallway. John replied, "I will come to the meeting tomorrow, and then I will go to du Tillet's home." Before Etienne could argue, he slipped out the door into the alley.

As John ran down the dark street, he heard rough voices demanding, "Open for the gendarmes!"

The next evening several men huddled around a single candle in a secret room. Somberly, a Belgian refugee told of the persecution of Christians in his town. The lame cobbler, Milon, spread his hands in a wide gesture.

"It will happen here," he said.

"We must defend ourselves before the King and all the people!" exclaimed a young man. John judged him to be little more than nineteen years old.

Etienne de la Forge shook his head. "We must not cause trouble. There are too many lives at stake.

Perhaps if we quietly spread the Gospel, God will raise up righteous leaders to protect us. Already, Princess Margaret intercedes for us before the King."

"What can she do?" the young man countered. "She is subject to every whim of the King. Most of the Christians that she sheltered have fled from Paris. It is not safe here."

Etienne exchanged a quiet glance with John. He turned to the young man. "We must not do anything rash."

A few weeks later, placards appeared all over Paris. There was even a placard outside the King's bedchamber. The placards denounced the Catholic Mass and boldly declared the Gospel.

The King and Parliament were outraged. They called for the immediate execution of those who were responsible. In four of the most public places, thirty-two people were burned at the stake.

John, who had returned to the home of du Tillet, realized that even his safe haven was in danger. Thus, on a chilly morning in 1534, John and du Tillet escaped over the French border into the Confederacy of Swiss States.

Ⅎ℁ℛ

John crossed the bridge over the wide Rhone river in the city of Basel. Chestnut trees lined the streets. Red geraniums filled the window boxes of the town houses. Storks nested in the gables.

John found a place to stay. He gave his name as *"Martinius Lucanius."* It was the Latin form of the name of Martin Luther, whom he admired.

Olivétan lived in Basel. John went to see him the first day.

Olivétan embraced his cousin. "This is one of my happiest days," he said. "I thank the Lord that He has brought you to salvation!"

John learned that Olivétan had been ministering to Christians in the Piedmont area of France since he last saw him.

"They call themselves Waldensians," explained Olivétan. "Three hundred years ago a man named Peter Waldo had parts of the Bible translated into French. There have been true believers there ever since."

Olivétan also told John about a Swiss city called Geneva. He had spent the last two years helping to plant the Reformation there.

"They are a brave and independent people. For a long time they were ruled by the Dukes of Savoy and the Catholic Church. When they decided to join the Reformation, they had to fight for independence. They tore down the half of the city that was outside of the wall and fortified their defenses."

"What happened?"

"The people made terrible sacrifices. Some even starved to death in the siege that followed. But in the end they won their freedom. They declared themselves to be a Reformation church."

THE PRINTSHOP

Olivétan introduced John to a man named Viret.
He had been a pastor in Geneva, too. Olivétan told
John that Viret was the most tenderhearted man he
had ever met, yet he was almost killed by a priest
several years ago.

"He still has the scar where the lance struck
him," said Olivétan.

John and Viret spent happy hours discussing the
Bible. Both men were passionate students of the
Bible. Viret often said, "You must meet my friend,
William Farel. He would love to talk with you."

John remembered Farel's name. He was the

fiery pastor in Meaux who had to flee when the persecution started. "I would like to meet him, too."

John soon learned that the people of Geneva were not the only people who were making great sacrifices. French refugees streamed into Basel when persecutions began in France. After the Affair of the Placards, dozens of Christians were arrested. Etienne de la Forge and the lame cobbler, Milon, were burned to death. John grieved with every piece of news.

John helped with preaching, counselling, visiting, comforting, and teaching among the Christian refugees. He helped Olivétan to edit the French Bible. He also worked on his manuscript to explain the Christian faith. As he mourned the persecutions in France, he decided to dedicate the manuscript to King Francis. John wrote:

> To his most Christian Majesty, Francis, King of the French and his Sovereign, John Calvin wisheth peace and salvation in Christ . . .
> Review, Sire, all the parts of our cause and consider us worse than the most abandoned of mankind unless you clearly discover that we thus "both labor and suffer reproach because we trust in the living God," because we believe that "this is life eternal to know the only true God and Jesus Christ, whom He hath sent." For this hope some of us are bound in chains, others are lashed with scourges, others are carried about

as laughingstocks, others are cruelly tortured,
others escape by flight . . .
Yet shall we in patience possess our souls and
wait for the mighty hand of the Lord, which
undoubtedly will in time appear and show itself
armed for the deliverance of the poor from their
affliction, and for the punishment of their
despisers, who now exult in such perfect
security. May the Lord, the King of Kings,
establish your throne with righteousness, and
your kingdom with equity.

John met the gray-haired printer, Thomas Plater, on a raw morning in winter. Thomas ran a bustling shop at the Sign of the Black Bear, where ten apprentices busily set type and ran the large presses.

Thomas liked the sincere young Frenchman and offered to print the manuscript.

"What will you call it?" he asked.

John hesitated. "I thought I might call it the *Institutes of the Christian Religion*, because it is about the most basic message of the Bible."

The printer nodded his approval. "That is a fine title and will catch the attention of many Bible scholars, I think." He went on to tell John that printers were working as fast as they could to keep up with the demand for Bibles. "Your cousin's Bible is selling faster than we can print them. And I have heard that Martin Luther completed his Bible translation into German. It will be all that we can do to keep up with the demand."

Olivétan and John spent long hours discussing the Bible. John detected a restlessness in his cousin.

"John, God has lit a fire in me, and I must return to France."

"But you will be killed if they find you," said John.

"The Bible says that the fear of man lays a snare. I cannot be content in Basel while my own countrymen are ignorant of the true faith. They will die without the gift of salvation being offered to them, unless someone goes."

John was quiet. He wished that Olivétan could be content with his ministry in Basel.

"John, don't you ever feel driven by God to proclaim His Gospel?"

John thought of the congregation in the cave by the river, the congregation in the wilderness, and the faithful people in Paris. He knew that he would gladly risk his life for them.

"I understand. I only wish that God was giving you an easier path."

"God's path is the best path," said Olivétan solemnly. The next week he left for France to minister again to the Waldensian Christians in the Piedmont area.

The first edition of the *Institutes of the Christian Religion* in Latin was published as a pocket-size book in March of 1536. The book was an instant success.

The time was ripe for John to pursue his dream of being a Christian scholar. He heard that the Duchess of Ferrara welcomed Christian scholars to her court. John left Basel and travelled to Ferrara, Italy.

The Duchess welcomed John warmly. John found that she was a dignified and intelligent women. She was the daughter of Louis XII and would have been rightful queen of France if women had been allowed to inherit the throne.

The Duchess met with John frequently for encouragement from the Bible. Her husband, however, remained an enemy of the "New Faith," as he called it. The day soon came when it was no longer safe in Ferrara. Rumors of poisonings and prison spread. With regret John left Ferrara.

John corresponded faithfully with his new friend throughout his life. His letters would prove a great encouragement during the years the Duchess was imprisoned for her faith and denied access to her own son.

John travelled to France. The king had extended a grace period for exiles to return to France for six months, in order to persuade them back to Mother Church. John used the opportunity to visit Paris and Noyon. As the last few days of the grace period approached, John started off for Strasbourg with his brother, Antoine, and half-sister, Marie.

Strasbourg was the German city that Olivétan had recommended to John many years ago. There was a flourishing French refugee community in the city. It would provide the appropriate setting for a scholar who sought a peaceful place to study.

For God does not consider, in chastening the faithful, what they deserve, but what will be useful to them in future, and fulfills the office of a physician rather than of a judge.

~ John Calvin

13

A DETOUR

The ride to Strasbourg started poorly. The route had to be changed because a large army of King Francis blocked the border to the German States. Their detour required them to go south, through the city of Geneva.

After several days of hard travelling, they were actually farther from their goal than at the beginning. Antoine and Marie remained as good-natured as ever, but John could tell that they were tired. John realized they could not hope to reach Geneva before sunset. It meant one more night on the road, but if they could find an inn all should be well. They would reach Geneva the next day, and could rest there for a few days.

When they did not reach an inn by sunset, John began to worry. He had heard grisly stories from the merchants of Basel about travellers caught unaware after dark. As they passed a dark thicket of trees, John wondered if there might be brigands lying in wait for them. What could they do if they were attacked?

With growing apprehension, John scanned the horizon for a hint of light from a town or inn. As he ascended the shoulder of a hill, he saw a faint glimmer. John urged the horses to go as quickly as they could. At last they reached the yard of a small inn.

The inn was crowded, but the innkeeper was glad to take a few more. John followed the man past black-handed charcoal burners who hunched over their drinks. The air smelled stale after riding all day in the July sun, but John knew this was the best they could find this night.

The innkeeper brusquely showed them to a room. It was scarcely big enough for the cot and crude wooden table that furnished it. John thanked the man and paid him for one night's stay. Then he beckoned to Antoine and Marie to enter the room. John set his sputtering candle on the table and carefully put his thin money wallet in an inner pocket of his overcoat. When the door was shut, he whispered to Antoine, "Did you secure the horses for tonight?"

"Yes," Antoine replied, "But you should have seen the disreputable fellow who keeps the horses here. I wouldn't be surprised if he tells us that our horses disappeared during the night when we go to fetch them tomorrow."

John smiled for the first time that evening. "Antoine, you are always imagining things. The Lord is sovereign over the sparrows. He can take care of us and our horses, too! The important thing is that we get some sleep. Marie, you take the cot. Antoine and I will sleep on the floor." Before John took his place he slid the wooden table against the door. He noticed Antoine watching him, so he tried to say as nonchalantly as possible, "Just in case, Antoine."

"And you're the one who thinks I'm imagining things," Antoine teased.

John would have launched a discussion of God's providence, but he felt his eyes closing in sleep. He could set Antoine straight tomorrow.

The new day dawned bright and sunny. Despite Antoine's fears, the horses were not stolen, and the worries of last night seemed far away. As John started on the southward journey, he gazed at the deep blue sky and breathed in the smell of freshly cut hay. "Next stop Geneva," he called out happily.

ഇരുഇരു

In Geneva, a man restlessly paced the floor of a church. A thatch of red hair framed his piercing eyes and sharp nose. His long beard gave him an air of weighty contemplation. His name was William Farel. He was a thin, sinewy man, whose small stature

93

belied his great physical stamina.

Farel had never been trained to be a priest like the great Martin Luther. His keen insight into the Bible and unusual zeal to make the Gospel known had resulted in his ordination as minister among Reformed churches. He gave all of his energy to the fledgling Christian community in Geneva. His flock loved him. They liked to brag that their minister had a fiery passion for God to match his red hair.

Farel had just finished his evening preaching and should have been home. Instead, he used these few free moments to pray for his congregation. He feared that the people were not being cared for adequately. The task was too large. He needed a well-trained scholar to help him educate his congregation. These people had been without the truth of the Bible for generations. The time was ripe to fully open the Bible to them.

He glanced at the small book in his hand. It was written by a Frenchman named John Calvin. Farel thought, "Here is a man who understands the Bible." He opened the book to read it once more. His heart warmed as he read the simple explanation of God's grace. It reminded him of a day many years ago.

It was a snowy February day in Dombresson, Switzerland. Farel was travelling with a small band of evangelists to churches in the area. They came to a church where the priest was saying Mass. They had originally planned to address the people after the service, but as the priest held up a wafer and proclaimed that it was the actual body of Christ that was at this moment being sacrificed again for the people, Farel could not restrain himself.

He stood up and called to the priest, "My poor brother, don't you realize that you are using the name of Jesus Christ blasphemously?"

The priest stopped at once and answered, "I did not know that I was blaspheming. If I am, I will stop."

Farel saw that he was sincere. He walked to the front of the church and said, "Give me your Bible and I will show you how you are completely renouncing the death and suffering of our Lord Jesus Christ." He opened the Bible, and continued, "Do you see here where it reads, 'He sacrificed himself for us once and for all,' and here again, it says, 'He does not need to sacrifice himself again.'"

As Farel read, tears began flowing down the cheeks of the priest. He could not speak at first. He took off his priest's robe and squarely faced his congregation. "I have made poor use of these," he said to the people. "Will you pray with me?" He fell to his knees, and began to pray. For the first time in his life he prayed in French, the language of the people. "Lord, I confess that I have made poor use of the office that you have given me. I ask for your forgiveness, and I promise that I will never say Mass again. By your strength and will, may the people here understand your truth, and may the idols that hinder us be knocked down."

Farel bowed his head as the priest prayed. When he looked up he saw that every person present was weeping. He later learned that many hearts were changed that day. The church itself was transformed. Even the statues of saints that people formerly prayed to were removed. The priest's prayer was answered beyond what Farel had imagined possible. And yet Farel had seen the same amazing changes taking place in town after town.

A door opened and the sudden rush of cool air brought Farel back to the Geneva of 1533. Farel recognized his visitor at once. "Viret," he greeted the man enthusiastically, "What brings you here at this hour?"

Viret smiled. "I see you are engrossed in Calvin's little book. How would you like to meet the author tonight?"

Farel reached for his friend's shoulder and gave him a firm grasp. "Are you saying that John Calvin is here in Geneva even as we speak?"

"Yes, and I know where he is lodging. We have often spoken of you, and I know he would love to meet you."

Farel grabbed his hat and ushered Viret out before he could say another word. "Take me to him at once," he ordered. Viret would have had a difficult time keeping up with him, had it not been necessary for Farel to allow him to lead the way. Farel felt that he could not reach Calvin's lodgings fast enough.

John was surprised to hear a knock at the door.

Besides Viret, he did not know anyone in Geneva. Marie opened the door for him. Viret embraced his old friend and introduced John to his red-headed companion.

"I have long wanted to meet you," John said warmly.

The two men talked long into the night. Farel told John of his work in Geneva. With great passion, he explained how Geneva was an important foothold for the true faith. John told Farel about the burden he carried for his countrymen in France and how he hoped to write books for them so that they could understand the Bible. John realized he had found a staunch friend.

John planned to stay in Geneva for three days. On his last night Farel came to see him. He talked to John with more than his usual energy. John listened quietly. Already his thoughts were fired with ideas for study and writing.

Farel paced the room as he talked. At last he stopped before John. He said in his thundering voice, "John, I burn with the zeal to advance the Gospel and I will strain every nerve to convince you to stay here."

John was startled. He shook his head firmly. "I am sorry, but my heart is set. I will devote myself to studying the Bible."

Farel persisted. "I understand your desire for private study, but your work on the *Institutes of the Christian Religion* betray your desire to communicate the Bible to other people. Please join me in the work in Geneva. You will be mightily used by God."

"I believe that God wants to use me to study and write about the Bible," John replied evenly.

Farel's eyes flashed. "You are following only your own wishes, and I declare, in the name of God Almighty, that if you do not assist us in this work of the Lord, the Lord will punish you for seeking your own interests rather than His!"

Whatever authority is exercised in the Church ought to be subjected to this rule: that God's law is to retain its own preeminence, and that men blend nothing of their own, but only define what is right according to the Word of the Lord.

~ John Calvin

14

GENEVA

John remained in Geneva. The councils of Geneva voted to call him to be preacher and professor of sacred literature. Alongside William Farel, he preached, ministered to the congregation, and performed a hundred other duties that must be done for a large congregation.

Geneva was certainly a large congregation. Every citizen was a member of the church. The preachers took turns preaching in the various church buildings at several services every Sunday and during the week. John barely took time to sleep. He also found new projects to keep him busy.

John petitioned the councils for permission to have the congregation sing. The people had not sung in church for centuries, but John had learned the value of song during his time with the underground churches in France.

John explained to the councils that the Bible taught, "Let the Word of Christ dwell in you richly in all wisdom; teaching and admonishing one another in psalms and hymns and spiritual songs, singing with grace in your hearts to the Lord." The councils approved.

John planned to teach the songs to the children first. They could lead the congregation in singing. He would teach them hymns that his old friend, Clement Marot, had composed. He even wrote a song for the children. It began:

> I greet thee, who my sure Redeemer art,
> My only trust and Saviour of my heart,
> Who pain didst undergo for my poor sake,
> I pray thee from our hearts all cares to take.

More than ever, John wanted to instruct young Christians in the faith. He wrote a catechism, urging believers everywhere to "long for the pure spiritual milk" of the Bible, and to be able to "give account of the hope that is in you."

In the catechism, he wrote

> We believe that all the elect are united in one Church, one communion, one people of God, whose prince and leader is our Lord, Christ . . .

Farel admired the catechism, but he was more practical. "How will you teach it to all the people?"

John smiled. "I have already begun."

"How?"

"I am beginning with the children. They will teach their parents."

That afternoon the children clustered in small groups in the great Cathedral of Saint Peter.

"Pierre says there will be a surprise today," said a boy with dark brown hair and eyes.

"What is the surprise?" asked a chorus of voices.

"Pastor Calvin will not tell anyone. He says we must learn our catechism first."

John entered, and a hush settled on the children. "Hello, little ones," he said cheerfully. "Are you ready for the lesson today?" The children eagerly stood to recite the answers to the catechism questions.

"What is faith?" John prompted them.

The children recited in unison, "Faith is a sure and steadfast knowledge of the fatherly goodwill of God toward us, as he declares in the Gospel that for the sake of Christ, He will be our Father and Saviour."

"Very good!"

John made a game of learning. He stopped frequently to explain the meaning of certain questions.

Finally he was satisfied that they knew their lessons. "I have a surprise for you," he told the children. "I am going to teach you a song that you

JOHN TEACHING THE CHILDREN

can sing in church for your parents."

The boy with the dark brown hair raised his hand. "Pastor Calvin, we cannot sing because we do not   know Latin."

"But you do not need to know Latin because this song is in French." A ripple of excited whispers went through the class. John raised his hand to get their attention. "Let me sing the song first, and then you can sing after me."

John began to sing in a clear tenor voice. His song echoed richly in the huge cathedral. It was not a monotonous song as the monks chanted. It was as lively as a folk tune. The children could not help joining their voices to his. They sang:

I greet thee, who my sure Redeemer art,
My only trust and Saviour of my heart . . .

With glowing eyes the children sang until they were breathless. "Where did you learn this song?" they asked.

"Someone who loves the Lord Jesus wrote it," John said.

ℰℭℛ

John studied the faces of the men at the large gathering. John and Farel were attending a week-long debate between Catholic and Protestant scholars. The citizens of Lausanne would choose to be either a Catholic or a Protestant city after this debate.

Lawyers in black gowns surrounded the Catholic

leaders in their rich velvet robes. Protestant leaders took their places, and set their thick Bibles before them. In the audience, monks of various orders and citizens thronged the church to hear the debate.

Farel nudged John. "You must not be shy today, John. We will need your knowledge and clear thinking to uphold the truth."

John smiled. "I doubt that I can add anything to what you will say, but I will be here if you need me."

For the first three days fiery Farel defended the truths of the Bible. Repeatedly, Farel's eyes met John's. He said silently, "Help me, John." But every time, John shook his head.

At the end of the third day John applauded Farel. "You are doing a fine job. You are mistaken if you think I can add anything to what you have said."

Farel shook his head in amazement. "You are trained as a lawyer. You cannot truthfully say that my defense of Christianity is as powerful as yours would be. If only you weren't so shy!"

On the fourth day a Catholic scholar by the name of Mimard read his speech. He declared that the Reformers were teaching the Lord's Supper in a way that went against the Bible and the early Church father, Augustine. A murmuring began among the audience. "Could it be that we are deceived?" some began to whisper.

Slowly, John rose to his feet. He looked intently at Mimard and began to defend the Reformers. "First, let it be understood that we, like all true believers, find August-ine to be in accord with the Bible. Before you condemn us, let me open the writings of Augustine for you."

John began to quote large sections of Augustine's writings from memory. The audience stopped their whisperings. In amazed silence they hung on John's every word. He not only quoted from Augustine, but from other early Church leaders. He also quoted from the Bible.

He turned to his audience. All shyness disappeared. "Judge for yourselves whether we are hostile to the Bible and the church fathers who knew it so well. As for the Lord's Supper, the Bible teaches that it is a spiritual communion that binds through a spiritual bond, the bond of the Holy Spirit. We confess our faith based alone on Holy Scriptures, without any additions from human wisdom."

As John sat down, the audience remained in stunned silence. The learned priests exchanged worried glances. None of them could attack John Calvin's words. He knew too much.

Suddenly, a Franciscan friar stood up. The people recognized him at once as Jean Tandy, one of the most outspoken opponents to the "New Faith." Today he was not the self-assured preacher who eloquently persuaded his congregation to stay with Mother Church.

"My friends," he began in a voice choked with emotion. "It is a sin to stubbornly rebel against the clear truth. I confess that I am guilty, because I have ignorantly lived in error and taught you lies. I ask God's forgiveness for everything I have wrongly taught, and I ask you to forgive me, too. I hereby defrock myself so that I may follow Christ and the truth of the Bible alone."

The audience was in an uproar. Within twenty-four hours, all the houses of sin had been closed in Lausanne. In the next few months, a growing number of the clergy converted to the "New Faith." Mimard himself became a Christian. When the time came for the citizens to vote, they overwhelmingly chose to become a Reformed city.

Afflictions are not evils, because they have glory annexed to them . . . We are not afflicted by chance, but through the infallible providence of God.

~ John Calvin

15

MY ONLY TRUST AND SAVIOR OF MY HEART

Back in Geneva, sunshine flooded the cramped office that John shared with Antoine. An open Bible lay before John as he wrote his *Instruction in Faith*. He wrote:

> *Prayer is similar to a communication between God and us whereby we expound to him our desires, our joys, our sighs, in a word, all the thoughts of our hearts.*

John sighed. He paused to gaze at the mountains that rose to the south of Geneva. He silently prayed for the people of Geneva. There had been so much conflict lately.

A knock sounded at the door and Farel strode into the room. "John, the Lord will call the Council to account for their actions!" he thundered.

John thought of the recent conflict. Farel and he had been called before the Council. The pastors testified that the power to decide who is fit for the Lord's Supper should belong to the church, not the government. "Did the Council decide against the church?" John asked

"It's worse than that," Farel said with a scowl. "Not only do they think the government should make all the decisions for the church, but they are forcing this on us!" He thrust a sealed letter into John's hand.

John scanned the letter. It declared that certain rituals would be added to the church.

John felt a rising anger. "How can they do this?"

"They claim that they must follow the urging of the Bern City Council."

"But this is politics they are pursuing, not the Word of God!"

Farel slumped in a chair, his rage spent. "It is the Libertines. They only voted for the Reformation because they wanted to be free of dukes and popes. They have no use for God and His church, and they will do everything they can to destroy it."

"But there are so many more citizens who are sincere Christians," began John.

Farel wearily shook his head. "They are good citizens, but they are afraid to speak out against the Libertines. The Libertines have power. They protest more loudly. They incite the rowdy youths to fire guns outside our doors."

John nodded grimly as he remembered the derision that such people poured on him when he walked the streets. Some Libertines even named their dogs "Calvin."

That day John and Farel protested to the Councils. They explained that in spiritual matters the Bible gave authority to spiritual leaders. The Council did not agree.

John's fellow preacher, a blind minister named Couralt, preached the next Sunday that the Council members were like "rats in the straw." When the soldiers put him in prison, John and Farel went to the Council to defend him. A crowd of Libertines jeered at them as they strode to the town hall.

"It is wrong to imprison a servant of God," John hotly declared. Tempers in the Council flared. The Council decided that if the pastors did not submit to the rituals of Bern, they could not preach or give the Lord's Supper.

The following Sunday, John prayed as he walked to the Cathedral of Saint Peter where he would serve that morning. Farel and he agreed that they must serve God rather than men. Solemnly, John preached to his flock. Farel, in the Church of the Rive, preached as well.

In the afternoon John spoke at the Church of the Rive. "We face troubles," he began, "but we must desire the Word of God as our only guide, not the additions of men."

Several men leaped forward with swords flashing. John's friends sprang in front of him. They formed a human shield. Amid the shouting and confusion, they escorted John to his home.

The next morning a sergeant delivered the resolution of the Council. The preachers were to be exiled. The Council decreed that they must leave Geneva within three days. As John read the resolution, he felt as though God were removing a huge burden from him.

"Please deliver this message to the Council," John told the sergeant. "If we had served men, we would have been poorly rewarded; but the Lord whom we serve thinks of His servants beyond measure!"

John made his way to Strasbourg while Farel went to serve the church in Neuchatel. John wrote to him there soon after:

> They suppose that the best course for them-selves to pursue was to tear in pieces our estimation, publicly and privately, so as to ren-der us as odious as possible. But if we know that they cannot calumniate us, excepting insofar as God permits, we know also the end God has in view in granting such permission. Let us humble ourselves, therefore, unless we wish to strive with God when He would humble us. Meanwhile, let us wait upon God.

In the dim light of evening, John searched the row of houses for the Bucer home. Antoine spotted it first. "There! The house with the light in the window," he said with relief.

John knocked on the heavy oak door. At once the door was thrown open. A small woman with rosy cheeks peered from behind the door. "May I help you?" she asked politely.

John spoke for the group. "I am John Calvin, and this is my brother, Antoine. We are looking for Martin Bucer. Is this his home?"

For an answer the woman smiled warmly. "You have come to the right place. Come in."

The moment John stepped into the room he felt at home. Like his childhood home in France, the kitchen served as the main room of the house. The air was heavy with the smell of soup and the fresh straw that was laid on the floor to keep feet warm. Their hostess directed them to sit on the wooden chairs near the stove. "I am Elizabeth Bucer, and I am pleased to meet you," she began. "My husband and the other members of our household will be home soon. They received word that you were coming." She smiled again. "I'm sure you will have a lot to talk about."

While John waited a little boy crawled onto the chair next to him.

"You must be the son of Martin Bucer," said

JOHN REMAINED IN STRASBOURG TO MINISTER TO THE GROWING
FRENCH CONGREGATION

John.

The boy nodded shyly. "Would you tell me a
story?"

he asked.

John thought for a moment. "Have you ever heard of the church that met in a cave?"

The boy's gray eyes opened wide. "No," he said breathlessly.

"There were some brave people who loved God, but their King said they must not meet to worship God. This made them sad. They knew if they met in one of their homes, the king's soldiers might see them and take them to prison. What do you think they did?"

The boy giggled in anticipation. "Did they meet in a cave?"

John looked surprised. "How did you know?" He continued, "When night fell, they would make their way quietly by the light of the moon to a cave that was hidden in the rocks. They worshiped God in the cave. They had to sing quietly so that no one would hear them. They had a few pieces of paper with parts of the Bible written on them. One of the men would read these. They also prayed. They wished they could hear more words from the Bible, but there was no one who could help them."

"I wish my Daddy could go to them," said the boy.

"There is more to the story. God heard the prayers of His people. One day he sent a man to help them."

"Was he very brave?"

"He wasn't very brave, but God made him strong

113

so that he could tell the people about God. He brought the people a lot more pieces of paper with parts of the Bible written on them. The people were happy."

"Did he stay there forever in the cave?"

John shook his head sadly. "No, he could not. One night the king's soldiers tried to capture him and he had to run away."

"Where did he go?"

"I have heard that he is in Strasbourg."

The boy studied John carefully. He was about to ask one more question, but his father entered the room. Martin Bucer greeted John warmly. The two men talked long into the night. His son did not get to ask his question that night.

Martin Bucer asked John to remain in Strasbourg to minister to the growing French congregation. The refugees of John's new church were zealous Christians. John served them passionately. He felt that at last he had found a home in the little Church of Saint Nicolas.

Christ leads his disciples by the hand to the cross, and thence raises them to the hope of the resurrection.

~John Calvin

16

STRASBOURG

John walked past several guild houses. He smelled the sharp smell of boiling fat from the soap maker's house. Next he passed the fullers, who washed and shrunk woven cloth. There were also the lorimers, who made bits for horses, and the paper-makers near the river.

John had visited the papermaker once. He used a watermill to beat old rags into a pulp. He put the pulp into a wooden frame and placed the frame into a large vat until the pulp was spongy. Then he pressed the sheets in a screw press.

The papermaker was proud of his work. He told John that paper was becoming cheaper than parchment. Parchment was made from sheep skins. It took over two hundred sheep skins to make a parchment Bible, but a paper Bible could be made from old rags. Rags were plentiful because the clothing of the dead were thrown away after the Black Plague ravaged a town.

An icy wind whipped John's cloak as he reached the French section of Strasbourg. He wrapped the thin cloak closer around his shoulders and studied the houses. Monsieur Stordeur had asked John to visit him this week. "Look for the house with the pink roses," he had instructed him.

John despaired as he saw that every window box on the street was filled with red geraniums. Perhaps he was on the wrong street. As he turned to leave, he noticed a tiny door tucked into the corner where two larger houses met. A small window competed for space with a window box that overflowed with pink roses.

A young woman answered the door. Two children peered shyly from behind her skirts.

"Madame Stordeur?" John asked.

She smiled as she recognized her pastor. "Pastor Calvin, thank you for honoring my husband's request. He will be glad to see you."

John waited in the living room while Madame Stordeur summoned her husband from his workshop. John admired the simple room. Roses bloomed in a blue bowl on the table. Starched white curtains framed the window. The two copper pots gleamed from constant scouring.

Jean Stordeur entered the room. He was a large man. He wore the apron of a carpenter. He greeted John with a firm handshake.

"Pastor, I asked you to come to my house because I am perplexed with many questions."

Madame Stordeur slipped quietly into a chair next to her husband. Though her modesty prevented her from asking questions, she listened intently. John saw in her eyes the maturity that was common to many refugees.

"I will help if I can," replied John.

The carpenter explained that his family was from Belgium. They were forced to leave their home when they became Christians. Like many people in the Strasbourg congregation, they had endured much hardship and persecution until they had found freedom to worship as Christians in Strasbourg.

"We feel a strong bond with the people of your congregation, however, we cannot agree with you on some things. The people who brought the Gospel to us taught us that there is another authority besides the Bible. There is the activity of the Holy Spirit in us."

John listened carefully. He replied, "The Bible clearly teaches us that the Holy Spirit is active in believers. It is the Holy Spirit that enables us to understand God's truth. We also know that the Holy Spirit spoke through men to write the Scriptures. But we must not separate the Spirit from the Word of Christ."

"But what if something that I feel leads me to believe that the Scriptures are wrong?"asked Jean.

"God tells us in the Bible that, 'All scripture is inspired by God and profitable for teaching, for reproof, for correction, and for training in righteousness.' We cannot disregard even one doctrine in it."

"What is the work of the Spirit then?"

John smiled. He relished this kind of discussion. "The Spirit does not create new and unfamiliar revelations which lead us away from the doctrine of the Gospel. Rather, the Holy Spirit seals the truth of the Bible in our minds," he explained.

"But isn't it an insult to subject the Spirit to Scripture when everything is subject to Him?"

"It is no dishonor to expect the Holy Spirit to be always the same and in every way consistent with Himself. After all, He wrote the Scriptures. True, if He was subjected to some other standard it might humiliate or restrict Him, but as long as He is compared with Himself how can He be dishonored? We should get great comfort in knowing that God never changes."

Jean was quiet. He seemed to be struggling with the new concept.

"Jean, if you want the Holy Spirit to be active in

your life, you must be all the more diligent to study the Scriptures. Read your Bible. Listen to the reading of Scripture at church. Every time you attend to God's Word, God is at work in you."

Jean Stordeur became one of the Bible's strongest supporters. John often heard him in earnest discussion with new believers, explaining how the Bible is our foundation.

One day Jean introduced his pastor to an old friend. "This is Paul Volsec," began Jean.

John interrupted. "Wait, I know that name. It is related to the book by Erasmus, called *The Manual of a Christian Soldier.*"

The man stepped forward and shook John's hand. "You must have a good memory. My friend, Erasmus, dedicated that book to me."

"Then I am delighted to make your acquaintance," said John. "In a way, Erasmus' idea of a Christian soldier started me on this path I tread today."

Paul Volsec laughed. "That is true for many of us. They say that Erasmus laid the egg, and Martin Luther hatched it!"

John's new friend was an unusually learned and perceptive man. Like Jean, he had many questions about the Holy Spirit's work. He studied the Bible under John's guidance. Like Jean, he became an ardent defender of the authority of the Bible. He could not know that one day he would be pastor of the little church where he first learned the pure doctrine of the Bible.

John served not only his own congregation, but many Christians who wrote to him. Some of the citizens of Geneva wrote to John for advice when strife continued to ravage the Genevan church. John wrote:

> Among Christians there ought to be so great a dislike of schism, as that they may always avoid it so far as lies in their power. That there ought to prevail among them such a reverence for the ministry of the Word and of the Sacraments, that wherever they perceive these things to be, there they may consider the Church to exist. Nor need it be any hindrance that some points of doctrine are not quite so pure, seeing that there is scarcely any Church which does not retain some remnants of former ignorance. It is sufficient for us if the doctrine on which the Church of God is founded be recognized and maintain its place.

One Sunday, John noticed that the Stordeur family was not in church. He knew that there must be a terrible crisis to keep the family from worship.

John ate a hasty noon meal and left to visit his parishioners. He went to the Stordeur home first.

Madame Stordeur met him at the door. Her face was white.

"Pastor, you must not come in here," she whispered hoarsely. "Jean has contracted the Plague."

"Please let me see him," John said.

Reluctantly, the young wife opened the door. John went at once to the side of his friend. The man, who had been so strong, could barely grasp John's hand. His face was bloated and blotched with gray spots. He breathed with effort. John had seen these symptoms before.

"Oh Lord," he prayed, "You are our Savior and Creator, and we put our lives into your hands. We beg for your compassion on Jean and his family. If it is your will, remove the Plague from this household."

As John continued to pray, Madame Stordeur sat tensely in her chair. John finished his prayer. He noticed how tired she looked.

"Would you like for me to sit with him so that you can rest?"

Madame Stordeur could not speak for a moment. John saw both anguish and exhaustion in her eyes. "I'm sorry, Pastor Calvin," she said quietly, "But I must be with my husband now."

"I will be praying for you," he replied. "And I will come tomorrow."

One by one, members of John's congregation

became sick. John did all that he could to comfort their suffering. Each time that he stood in his pulpit, he noticed the absence of more people. He prayed fervently to God to remove this curse.

The words of Job came to John's mind: "Shall we receive good at the hand of God, and shall we not receive evil?"

Jean Stordeur died on a summer morning. John grieved with Madame Stordeur and her two children. He thought of the many people that he loved who were already with God: de la Forge, Milon, and other Christians of Paris who were martyred for their faith. John prayed, "Lord, put bounds to our grief so that we are not overcome."

Christ, giving himself to us, invites us not only by his example to give ourselves and to expose ourselves mutually one for the other, but inasmuch as he makes himself common to all, he makes us also all one in himself.

~ John Calvin

17

THE CHURCH OF SAINT NICOLAS

The rosy light of dawn lit the way as John walked to the Church of Saint Nicolas this Sunday morning. As was his habit, he did not eat breakfast so that his mind would be clear. John sat on one of the wooden benches and prayed while the sun rose higher in the blue sky.

Soon a family entered at the solid oak door. The father led them to a bench. Before they sat, they bowed their heads and prayed. More families entered. As the bells of Strasbourg rang nine times, John rose and called the people to worship. The congregation sang:

Thou shalt have no other gods before the Lord,
Thou shalt not make unto thee any graven

image,
Thou shalt not take the name of the Lord thy
God in vain,
Remember the sabbath day, to keep it holy.
Amen.

John prayed for God to give them understanding of the scriptures. Skirts rustled and benches creaked as the people stood to hear the Bible read. They stood to show their respect for the Word of God.

When the congregation was seated, John explained each verse of the reading in turn. He spoke simply so that the children could understand, too. John spoke from memory. As he preached, he looked over the congregation. The boys and girls forgot to fidget. They met his friendly gaze and did their best to remember everything their pastor said.

John closed the worship service with prayer. In unison, the believers prayed the Lord's Prayer. The children sang the loudest when it was time to sing the Apostle's Creed, which their pastor had taught them.

John spent the afternoon visiting people in their homes. So many persecuted Christians arrived in Strasbourg each week, that he could barely keep up with the new faces. The children in his catechism class begged for visits, too. When John arrived home, the sun was already setting in a scarlet ball over the steeple of the Church of Saint Nicolas.

John settled himself on a bench in the cozy Bucer home. People called their home the "Inn of

Righteousness." After two years in Strasbourg, John understood the title. Elizabeth Bucer cheerfully welcomed dozens of visitors each week. There was always a place for John. Although he was busy with his growing congregation, he enjoyed dinners in the Bucer home as often as he could.

Tonight the cares of the French and Belgian refugees who attended his church wore heavily upon him. John sat quietly while the other pastors and guests talked. Elizabeth dashed between the table and the kitchen to serve the guests. As she passed, she deposited the youngest of the five Bucer children on John's lap.

"Could you hold this little one for me?" she asked without waiting for an answer.

John cradled the baby. He remembered holding little Marie, and how his father had told him he must care for her one day. Now Marie was a married woman.

The other children clustered around John's chair. "Tell us a story," they begged.

"The one about the church in the cave," said the eldest daughter. John told the story once again. When John finished, the children sighed with satisfaction. One of the children said, "And you were the minister in the cave."

The baby gave a little cry and John busily tried to distract him. He bounced the baby a little. The baby smiled.

"John, you need a wife," said Martin Bucer in his

booming voice.

John felt himself turning red.

"That is right," said one of the young pastors. "Look how happy Martin is with his family."

"It would be good for your health, too," said Elizabeth. She felt responsible for the young men who worked with her husband.

"I doubt that any woman would have me," replied John. "My standards are too high."

Martin eyed John as though measuring him for a new coat. "Hmm. You might have to simplify your standards, but you must have a wife." John wondered if the decision was really that easy to make.

Over the next few weeks Martin worked at finding a wife for John. He found the perfect match for John, but she was unwilling to learn French.

A few months later he found another suitable prospect. John wrote to his friend William Farel to ask him to perform the marriage ceremony. Unfortunately, the young woman was not as suitable as John's friends had thought at first.

The difficulties embarrassed John. He decided to stop his search for a wife.

One sweltering summer day at the end of June, Martin Bucer burst into John's study. "I have good news for you! I have found the perfect wife."

John calmly looked up from a commentary he was writing. "Are you saying you have found a woman who would marry me?"

"I'm sure she would if you authorize a proposal.

She is the kind of woman you are looking for: virtuous, godly, and caring."

John was interested despite himself. "What is her name?"

"She is a member of your congregation. Do you know the widow, Madame Stordeur?"

At once the solemn face of Madame Stordeur came to John's mind. He remembered her quiet grief at her husband's death. He realized that in all her suffering her faithfulness at worship had never wavered. She possessed the strength of character that he sought in a wife.

"Please make the proposal," John said firmly. "I will eagerly wait for the answer."

John Calvin married Idelette de Bure, the widow of Jean Stordeur, on August 10, 1540. He brought her and her two children to his home in the French section of Strasbourg. At last the pastor of the Church of Saint Nicolas had a wife.

The purification of the Church is God's own work.

~ John Calvin

18
MY HEART TO GOD

"We thank you Lord for this food and for your many provisions to our family. Please sustain us with this food and the power of your Word. In our Savior's name, Amen."

John concluded his prayer and looked around the table at his new family. Idelette was flushed from the heat of the cook stove. When she smiled at John, his heart swelled with pride. In the few weeks since they were married, she proved to be a quiet strength to his life. She brought beauty to the bare parsonage. She shared his burdens. She shared his love for the Lord.

Next to Idelette sat Charles. He gulped his stew and bread with great concentration. He was twelve years old and always hungry. John hoped that he would be a strong young man like his father. Judith sat primly next to John. She was a miniature of her mother. She seldom spoke.

The young students who boarded with the Calvins filled the remainder of the broad table. Most of them were preparing for the ministry, but there was one boy who was younger than the rest. His father was an old friend and had asked John to raise his son while the boy attended school in Strasbourg. John loved him as a son. He wrote glowing reports to the boy's father about his progress in school.

Idelette filled John's cup and asked, "How was your day, John? I heard that you visited the LaVoie family today."

"I did, and it was the highlight of my day. They send their regards. They could not thank you enough for the help you gave when their baby was sick. She is healthy now." Idelette glowed with happiness and spoke a silent prayer of thanks.

"Papa," quavered a little voice at John's elbow.

John turned to his stepdaughter. "Yes, Judith."

"Is it true that each of us is protected by an angel?"

John peered into her serious little face and answered her solemnly. "It is certainly true, because the Bible tells us so. But I will tell you what I have found in my studies." John lowered his voice and leaned closer to Judith. "God says that he sends his 'angels' to watch over us. That means there is not just one, but many! That is the kindness of our God." Judith smiled shyly.

The next week John was required to attend a

conference of the church. He hated to leave his family, but Martin Bucer insisted that John's knowledge and speaking skills were needed to defend the Reformation.

John renewed his friendship with his old friend Philip Melanchthon. He was twelve years older than John, and had labored for many years at the side of Martin Luther. Like John, he had distinguished himself as a scholar at a young age. Wittenburg had appointed him as professor of Greek when he was only twenty-one years old. John thought that Philip was a man of incomparable knowledge, piety and other virtues.

John confounded the Catholic theologians with his enormous knowledge of the Bible and the church fathers. Melanchthon dubbed John "The Theologian." When he returned to his home, he showed one of John's booklets to Martin Luther. The booklet was a simple explanation of the Lord's Supper. Though Martin Luther did not agree with other Swiss Reformers on this issue, he exclaimed, "If my opponents and I had entrusted the whole affair of this controversy to Calvin, we should soon have been reconciled!"

During the conference the Black Plague returned to Strasbourg. John agonized over the safety of his family. He dispatched a note to Idelette to go to her brother's home outside the city. They safely weathered the Plague, but the young boy who boarded in the Calvin home died.

John felt as though he had lost his own son. He wrote to the grieving father:

He is one, who, having set sail upon the stormy ocean, is summoned back into port before he reached the open sea. Nor have I wished thee not to grieve. We do not learn a philosophy in the school of Christ which would have us suppress all those feelings which God has given us and turn men into stones. All that we have said is only to this end, to persuade thee to set a term to thy grief, and to assuage it; that when thou pourest out thy heart in tears, as nature and fatherly love dictate, thou mayest not altogether resign thyself to grief.

John and Idelette had been married for just over a year when the Council of Geneva asked John to return. John declined the call, but the people of Geneva insisted that only John could fill their need. In the three years since they banished their ministers, Geneva had been shepherded by weak men. Lawlessness increased. The people were desperate for order and godly leadership. They issued the call to John again and again.

John paced the floor of Martin Bucer's office. He told Martin of the call to Geneva. "I feel as though I have been given a sentence of death. I would rather face a thousand deaths than return to the trials we faced in Geneva."

Martin sat at his desk. His Bible lay open before him. "I read the commentary on Romans that you just published. You have a gift for explaining God's Word."

Usually John would have savored the compliment from his mentor, but he knew Martin had more to say.

Martin continued. "It says here in Romans that, 'Faith cometh by hearing, and hearing by the Word of God.' It also says, 'How shall they hear without a preacher?'"

"But the people there do not want a preacher! There is a large group that would destroy the true church if they could."

"Perhaps you are expecting too much of people who do not yet have faith. You should not be surprised at the actions of unbelievers. You must pray for them, and you must preach to them."

William Farel also wrote to urge John to return to Geneva. John wrote to him: "If I had any choice I would rather do anything than give in to you in this matter, but since I remember that I no longer belong to myself, I offer my heart to God as a sacrifice."

John drew a picture of a hand holding out a heart. It would be his emblem. He wanted to show that he had given his heart to God.

The wagon wheels transmitted every bump in the road as John rode to Geneva. John went ahead of the family so that he could set up their household. A battle still waged in his heart during the lonely journey, even after the warm greeting he received from the Genevan Council.

The Council provided a home for John at Number 11 Canon Street. It was only a block from the Cathedral of Saint Peter, where John would chiefly preach.

John walked the hill to the church for his first service. The majestic stone structure with its wooden steeple stood just as he had left it. The bells, affectionately called Clemence and Bellerive by the Genevans, still rang to call the people to worship. John mounted the steps to the pulpit and read his text. He began at the exact point where he had left off three years ago. The people, who remembered John's last sermon, stirred in their seats. The pastor acted as though he had never left. John looked into the faces of the men and women of Geneva. He realized that in his heart, he had never left them.

The fruit of the womb is not born by chance, but is to be reckoned among the precious gifts of God.

~ John Calvin

19
CHILDREN

At the house on Canon Street, pink roses bloomed in the window boxes. Crisp white curtains billowed softly at the open window. In the garden, Idelette filled her apron with beans and squash from from her small vegetable plot. She paused to look down the hill to the sparkling waters of Lake Geneva. Nearby, Judith and her two small cousins held hands and sang "On the bridge of Avignon, people dance . . . ."

In his study, John listened to the children's laughter while he prepared his next sermon. Suddenly the chatter of children's voices spilled up the stairway and into John's study.

"Papa," said Judith breathlessly, "we are playing school, and Samuel and John want you to give them their church lesson."

Samuel and John were Antoine's sons. Though

A VIEW FROM THE HOUSE ON CANNON STREET

they were too young for real school, Judith, who was ten, liked to pretend to be their teacher. She taught them to count on their fingers and say their letters.

John heard uneven steps on the stair. Anna, who was two, struggled up the last step after her brothers. She climbed onto John's knee and announced, "Me, too."

John glanced at his sermon. "Today I will tell you the story of a man named Saul. He thought he would please God by putting Christians in prison, but he did not really understand that Jesus was God's

Son. One day he was travelling to a city called Damascus, and Jesus spoke to him. Saul realized that he had been wrong. He believed in Jesus and spent the rest of his life serving God in the right way. God changed Saul."

"Why?" asked four-year-old John.

"Ah my little one, understanding the power of God is like a fly trying to eat all the mountains."

John's nephews looked doubtfully out of the window at the immense mountains.

"But why wasn't Saul good from the beginning?" asked Samuel.

John thought for a moment. "None of us is born good. It is as though we were all born lions, tigers, wolves, and bears. Do you know what they are like?"

For an answer the two boys growled and made their hands look like claws.

"Very good," said John. "That is the way we are born. But then the Spirit of Christ tames us and makes wild savage beasts into mild sheep."

"Baa," said Anna. John and the children burst into laughter.

After the children left, John resumed his studies. He did not notice that the hour grew late until he heard the sound of the front door closing. He looked out the window to see Idelette walking up Canon Street with the water pail in her hand. John watched her slim form walk slowly up the hill to the water fountain. Something about her gait looked different. He must remember to ask Idelette if she was well.

The bells chimed the hour and John gathered his papers for a Council meeting.

The men of the Council sat stiffly in their chairs. The clerk read the minutes of the meeting. One syndic rose and explained that John Calvin would present a proposal of "Ecclesiastical Ordinances." The Little Council and Council of Two Hundred had agreed that there should be a settled government for the church.

Carefully John read the papers before him. He explained the need for the church to have ministers, elders, and deacons like the New Testament church described in the Bible. He also read ordinances about baptism, the instruction of children, and the Lord's Supper.

As John walked home from the meeting, he prayed that the leaders would approve the ordinances. When he arrived at home, he found Idelette was already in bed.

John felt a pang of worry. Could Idelette be sick? But when he asked her, Idelette smiled her quiet smile. "I am only a little tired because we are expecting a baby."

John wrapped her in a warm embrace. "What a blessing," he murmured. His heart warmed to think that God had blessed them with a child.

Meanwhile, the Genevan Councils signed the Ecclesiastical Ordinances that John recommended. With the sound of trumpet and bell, the Little and Great Councils called together the people of Geneva.

On November 20, 1541, the people approved the ordinances.

The Black Plague came to Geneva, and a minister had to be chosen to attend to the dying in the hospital which lay outside the city. The first pastor volunteered, but he was soon struck with the Plague and died. John offered to go next. The Council, however, forbade him. "You are needed for the work of the church and could not be easily replaced," they explained. Idelette, who would deliver their baby in only a few months, wept with relief that John was spared.

The Plague raged throughout Europe. John received news that Elizabeth Bucer and four of her children died from the Plague. John thought of the "Inn of Righteousness," and the children who used to clamor for stories from him. He prayed for comfort. But another sadness was yet to come.

A few weeks later, Idelette delivered their infant son prematurely. They named him Jacques. John prayed earnestly for the lives of his wife and son, who were both in serious danger. Though Idelette slowly recovered, Jacques lived only fourteen days.

John poured out his grief to his old friend Viret in a letter:

The Lord has certainly inflicted a severe and bitter wound in the death of our infant son. But He is Himself a father, and knows what is good for His children.

In the darkness of our miseries,
the grace of God shines more brightly.

~ John Calvin

20

NO COMMON
SOURCE OF GRIEF

The years flew by as John ministered to his flock in Geneva and wrote on behalf of his flock in the world. John admired Martin Luther and attended many conferences in an effort to unite the German and Swiss churches. John often told his friends, "Remember what a great man Luther is." He liked to point out how bravely and firmly Luther labored, and how marvelously God had gifted him to explain the doctrine of salvation.

John wrote to Martin Luther:

Would that I could fly to you, that I might even for a few hours enjoy the happiness of your society . . . but seeing that it is not granted to us on earth, I hope that shortly it will come to pass in the Kingdom of God. Adieu, most renowned Sir, most distinguished minister of Christ, and my ever-honored father. The Lord himself rule and

direct you by his own Spirit, that you may perse-
vere even unto the end, for the common benefit
and good of his own Church.

When Martin Luther died in 1546, the Reformed churches increasingly looked to the pastor of Geneva for leadership. In 1547, Edward VI succeeded to the throne in England. He wanted to continue the reformation of the English churches. The Duke of Somerset was his regent since the king was not old enough to rule alone. The Duke wrote frequently to John for advice.

In October 1548, John wrote to the Duke of Somerset. He encouraged him to find godly preachers to serve the churches. He wrote:

Now, this preaching ought not to be lifeless but
lively . . . that the Spirit of God ought to sound
forth by their voice, so as to work with mighty
energy. And . . . if you desire to build an edifice
which shall be of long duration, and which shall
not soon fall into decay, make provision for the
children being instructed in a good Catechism,
which may show them briefly, and in language
suited to their tender age, wherein true
Christianity consists.

Idelette was a faithful partner to John in his ministry. She ran the busy household which now included not only her daughter, Judith, but Antoine's family with their four children. Idelette's son, Charles, was old enough to be apprenticed to his uncle in Strasbourg. During the next five years she bore two more children, who died in childbirth. Idelette and John shared the deep sadness of these losses.

One day Dr. Textor visited John. "John," he said, "I need to talk with you about Idelette." The doctor's tone was serious. At once John knew that something was wrong.

"I know that she has not recovered from the death of our little daughter," John began.

Dr. Textor shook his head sadly. "It is more than that. Idelette is very sick. I'm afraid that she will not recover."

John sank into a chair. He could barely comprehend the words. Idelette would not recover? How could there be a world without Idelette? John heard Dr. Textor talking as though from a distance. "I will do what I can, but you must encourage her to rest."

As the gray days of February turned to March, Idelette grew weaker. She could no longer walk the distance to the fountain to fetch water. She coughed frequently. Sometimes she coughed blood.

One morning Dr. Textor summoned John to come home. "I'm sorry, John," he said. "I'm afraid your wife does not have much longer to live."

John rushed to Idelette's bed. He tenderly took her hand in his. "You know that I will care for your children as if they were my own," he said softly.

Idelette's eyes filled with tears as she replied, "I have committed them to the Lord."

"But you must not hinder me from doing my duty, darling," John answered. Idelette tried to speak, but a fit of coughing seized her. John waited for the coughing to stop, then he began to pray for the children.

When he finished, Idelette's face shone. "If the

Lord shall care for them, I know they will be commended to you." John was overcome with grief. Idelette's selflessness was so great, that she seemed to have already left the world.

During the long afternoon, Idelette's pain increased. She wanted to speak, but could only gasp out short sentences. "O glorious resurrection! O God of Abraham and of all our fathers, in thee have the faithful trusted during so many past ages, and none of them have trusted in vain. I also will hope."

Her last words were, "Let us pray, let us pray. All pray for me." Then she lost the ability to speak.

John sat beside her bed and whispered to her of the happiness she had brought him, the love of Christ, and the hope of eternal life. Then he broke down and wept. Idelette looked at him with her soft, patient eyes. John clasped her hands in his and prayed.

Idelette passed away so calmly that those present could scarcely distinguish her life from her death.

John still clasped her hand.

John wrote to his old friend, Viret:

You know well how tender, or rather, soft, my mind is. Had not a powerful self-control been given to me I could not have borne up so long. And truly mine is no common source of grief. I have been bereaved of the best companion of my life, of one who, had it been so ordained, would have willingly shared not only my poverty, but even my death. During her lifetime she was the faithful helper of all my ministry.

Ambition deludes men so much
that by its sweetness it not only
intoxicates but drives them mad.

~ John Calvin

21

CONFLICT

John stood in the pulpit of the Cathedral of Saint Peter. He looked into the eyes of the men, women, and children as he delivered his sermon from memory. He saw the poor sitting beside the rich, councilmen beside other citizens. In Geneva there was no distinction.

John spoke: "Let us learn to know in everything and by everything the inestimable goodness of our God. For as He declared His love toward mankind when He spared not His only Son, but delivered Him to death for sinners, also He declares a love which He bears especially toward us when, by His Holy Spirit, He touches us by the knowledge of our sins and He makes us wail and draws us to Himself with repentance."

Although John grieved for Idelette, he did not allow himself to rest from his work. He buried himself in service to those who needed him. Christians from all over the world wrote to him for advice.

John corresponded with Thomas Cranmer, who was the Archbishop of Canterbury. Cranmer labored to reform the English church, and considered John his "very dear brother in Christ."

When a new believer wrote to John, he gave his reply the same careful attention that he gave to the Archbishop's letter. He wrote to the young man:

> *As I understand from your letter, that it is not very long since the Lord shed the light of His Gospel on you, I could not give a fitter expression of my love towards you, than by exhorting and encouraging you to daily exercises . . . For if you make a constant study of the Word of the Lord, you will be quite able to guide your life to the highest excellence.*

When five young missionaries to France were imprisoned for their faith, John pled their case with men of influence in France. He also wrote faithfully to the young men during their year of imprisonment. He supplied quotes from the Bible and the church fathers for them to use in their defense. He wrote to comfort and encourage them to hold fast to their faith.

Although the Swiss churches sent men to plead the cause of these faithful Christians, the French judge ruled that they must be burned at the stake.

John tenderly wrote his last letter to the five young men:

> *You know, however, in what strength you have to fight: a strength on which all those who trust, shall never be daunted.*

One afternoon John walked along the sparkling waters of Lake Geneva with Antoine's six children. They still spent most of their time in John's home, though the family had a villa outside Geneva. Samuel, the oldest, had bright, laughing eyes like his father. "Uncle John, tell us about the five missionaries who died for their faith."

John sighed and looked across the lake in the direction of France, his homeland. He began, "There were five young men who loved the Lord so much that they wanted to take the Gospel to their own country of France."

"But they were caught, weren't they?" interrupted Dorothy, John's youngest niece.

"Yes, and they gave a good account of their faith. Despite all that could be done, they were sentenced   to death."

Anna, who was tenderhearted, began to cry. "Please Uncle John," she said, "tell us what they said at the end."

John took his niece's hand as they walked. He continued, "As they were led to the stake, the five young missionaries sang psalms and repeated Bible verses. Martia Alba, who was the eldest, was the last to be tied to the stake. As he embraced each of the others, he said, 'Adieu, adieu, my brother.'

"The fire was kindled. 'Courage, my brothers; courage,' the young men exhorted one another in the midst of the flames. They were faithful to God to the end."

The children were quiet for a moment.

Samuel said, "If they burn Reformers in France, why don't we burn Catholics here?"

"No, Samuel, your parents, my parents, we all were Catholics once. What if we had been burned? We could never learn the truth from the Bible and come to our Lord Jesus in faith. We must teach those who do not have the Gospel yet. You must learn all you can so that one day you can take the Bible to those who are starving for it. Could you imagine the blessing if one day all Catholics had Bibles, too?"

Anna squeezed John's hand and skipped merrily beside him.

"We will take the Bible to everyone we can," said Samuel stoutly.

John felt driven to preach and write so that others might understand the Bible and grow in their faith. He wanted God's people to understand that their faith touched every point of their lives. A man did not have to be a preacher to devote himself to God. He liked to say: "God is our creator, and all of our life belongs to Him."

The Libertines, however, continued to flaunt the authority of the Bible in their lives. Their stubborn opposition to God distressed John. He visited several of their homes, but they insulted him and would not listen to him. John had to ask one man not to partake of the Lord's Supper because the man would not repent and give up his sinful lifestyle. At that moment, the battle lines were drawn.

When a man named Michael Servetus came to Geneva to challenge John Calvin, the Libertines championed his cause. Servetus had written a mocking book called *The Restitutes*, against John's *Institutes of the Christian Religion*.

Servetus was not a stranger to John. Even the sound of his name took John back to a day many years ago. It was Paris during the dangerous times before the Affair of the Placards. Etienne de la Forge was urging John to flee Paris before he was caught, but a young Spanish doctor named Michael Servetus requested an appointment with the underground preacher.

John remembered how eagerly he kept that appointment. Servetus was known by the underground church as a fellow rebel, yet he held unusual ideas about the Bible. Etienne thought the meeting was a trap.

"The authorities would gladly burn this Servetus. They will be tracking him and arrest you, too!" he told John.

"But he has asked me to meet him," countered

John. "Perhaps he is hungry for the Gospel."

"John, Servetus cannot be trusted. He boldly denies that Jesus is God. He only wants to debate you. Even you cannot convince such a man of the true Gospel." Despite the advice of his old friend, John decided that he must keep the appointment.

John knocked quietly at the door. A servant girl admitted him and directed him to sit in the front room. John waited. An hour passed. He began to feel uneasy. Perhaps Etienne was right. Perhaps it was too dangerous to remain in Paris. Was this a trap? John waited another hour, but Servetus did not come.

Though Servetus did not keep the appointment, he later corresponded with John. John wrote letter after letter in an attempt to convince him of the authority of the Bible, but Servetus refused to believe. He became more and more violent in his attacks against John.

Eighteen years after the failed meeting in Paris, the Catholic church arrested Servetus for the heretical beliefs he had published. They tried him and condemned him to be burned as a heretic. Servetus escaped before the execution. He boldly entered Geneva. The Genevan Council arrested him. They asked John to attend the trial.

When John entered the room, Servetus began to rail against him and call him names. "Wretch, wretch!" he yelled at John.

John stood before him without saying a word.

He thought of his real purpose. He was not in Geneva to defend his own honor. Only God's Kingdom mattered.

Servetus drew himself to his full height and pointed an accusing finger at John. "I will repeat again what I wrote to the Council on the twenty-second of September," he intoned in a voice of doom. "I demand that my false accuser be punished, and that he, like me, be imprisoned until the trial be decided either by his or my death or by some other punishment." He continued to rave, demanding that Calvin's property be given to him.

At that one councilman laughed and said, "That would be an easy prospect! Our minister keeps nothing for himself!"

The trial lasted several days. When John received news that the Council had given Servetus the death penalty, he did everything he could to lessen the penalty. He asked all the preachers to sign a petition of moderation. The Council, however, would not consider his petition.

John asked if he could see Servetus. He cherished one last hope of bringing the heretic to true salvation. When Servetus saw John he asked him for forgiveness.

John grasped the prisoner's hand. "Believe me, I never wanted you prosecuted because of some offense against me. Do you remember how I risked imprison-ment and death in France to meet you in Paris nineteen years ago? I wanted to win you to our

Lord then, and all those years I faithfully answered your letters to me.

"Are you thinking of asking forgiveness of the everlasting God whom you have blasphemed so many times? Would you like to be reconciled to the Son of God?"

Servetus shook his head. Though the prospect of death humbled him, he stubbornly stuck to his heretical views.

*We must see to it that the pulling down of error
is followed by the building up of faith.*

~ John Calvin

22
A STRANGER

In the dark morning hours, snow swirled around the Cathedral of Saint Peter. John worked by candlelight in the tower room. He wore his heavy cloak and flat velvet hat to keep out the chill. He quickly leafed through a pile of letters and papers. There was the letter to the King of Poland that must be finished. Also, the churches of Strasbourg, Frankfurt, and Wesel were waiting for his letters. He wanted to dedicate his commentary on Genesis to the three sons of Prince Johann Friedrich of Saxony. Then there were the printers waiting on his approval of several reprints and translations.

John cut a quill pen with his penknife and dipped the pen in ink. He began to write. He paused from his work to consider the needs of the Waldensian Christians. They had escaped from

153

France several years ago when entire communities of these humble believers were slaughtered by decree of the King of France.

A knock on the door startled John. He wondered who could be visiting so early in the morning.

John opened the door. He saw a stranger. He was medium height with broad shoulders. Dark blue eyes studied John intently. His black hair and thick beard gave him a wild look. Mud spattered his cape and boots, as though he had just taken a long journey.

"Monsieur Calvin? I was told I might find you here. I rise early. I hope you do not mind?"

"Not at all," replied John. "I am afraid I have not had the honor of making your acquaintance. Are you newly come from France? There is something about your French accent that is different."

The man laughed heartily. With a twinkle in his eye, he said, "I will tell you who I am after you guess where I am from."

John cocked his head to one side and studied the man. "Your clothes are from the north of France, but your accent is more typical of the west of France. One of the port cities perhaps."

"I congratulate you. I have recently come from Dieppe in the north of France where I acquired the clothes. As for my French accent, I learned it from sailors in the galleys of a French ship."

John smiled broadly. "I think I can guess your name, too. You are John Knox."

The man looked surprised.

It was John's turn to laugh. "I have heard of your work with the believers in Dieppe this year. I have wanted to meet you."

John spoke with his new friend about the needs of the English-speaking church in Geneva. Knox told John his story of persecution in his homeland of Scotland.

Knox asked John if a majority of believers would be justified in overturning an evil ruler. John thought of the horrors inflicted on godly men and women in his own country. He fingered the pages of the Bible that he always kept before him. He thought of the words of the Bible: "Let every soul be subject unto the higher powers. For there is no power but of God; the powers that be are ordained of God."

John met the penetrating stare of his new friend. "No, I do not believe that would be God's will."

Though the men did not agree on this topic, they found that they shared a burning passion for their Lord and Savior, Jesus Christ. Both men devoted every fiber of their being to ministering the Word of God to the world. Knox promised to return to Geneva one day.

In 1555, three hundred English Protestants were burned at the stake when the Catholic Queen Mary ascended to the throne. Hundreds of believers fled England. John Knox was called to serve one group of refugees in Frankfort.

Knox kept a regular correspondence with John during his years in Frankfort. When Knox disagreed with a faction of the church that wanted to keep some of the props of the Catholic church, John agreed with him. Nevertheless, he urged Knox to come to peace with his brethren.When it appeared that Knox and several others would leave the church, John wrote:

> When I heard that a part of you intended to quit your present residence, I carefully admonished them, as was my duty, that if it was not conve- nient for all to inhabit the same place, yet that separation to a distance should not break up your fraternal union . . . I greatly desire that what I hear of your return to mutual good will is solid and stable, that if any of you chance to wander elsewhere, though separated by place you can cultivate a holy friendship.

Knox returned to Geneva, where he continued to serve English-speaking people in exile. One member of his church was named John Foxe. He had a plan to record the stories of Christian martyrs. Another member was William Whittingham, who was translating the Bible into English. It would be called the Geneva Bible. It became the primary English Bible for the next century, even accompanying the Pilgrims across the ocean to America.

A few years later Knox received the call to return to Scotland to lead the Reformation there. Knox was reluctant to leave the congregation which he served in exile. He also knew that the path to Reformation in Scotland would lead to heartache and trials. Knox appealed to John.

John sat at his desk with his Bible open before him. Knox paced the room. He ran his fingers through his black hair so that it stood on end.

John remembered a similar scene many years ago, when he had been the pacing man.

"My friend," John said quietly, "you have received a gift from God and now you are being called to use it for God's Kingdom in Scotland."

"But I can use it in Geneva just as well," replied Knox.

"You have been faithful here and there is already much fruit, but how will the people of Scotland hear unless they have a preacher?"

Knox's eyes snapped blue sparks. "I know I must go, but I fear that I am not capable of this work. Why is God calling me back?"

"Let us pray," replied John. The two men bowed their heads. They poured out their hearts before their

Lord, who had called both men to works that were greater than their human abilities.

As he closed in prayer, Knox whispered, "Give me Scotland, or I die. Amen."

When John next heard from Knox, amazing changes were taking place in Scotland. The people thronged to hear the Bible preached. Churches declared themselves to be Reformation churches in a single day. Through years of turmoil, sacrifice, and the mighty work of God, Scotland became a Protestant nation.

Soli Deo Gloria
(To God alone the glory)

~ John Calvin

23

I GREET THEE WHO MY SURE REDEEMER ART

The clatter of hammers and chisels mingled with the grunts of men as they lifted heavy stones into place. John stood in the midst of the dust and noise and imagined how the building would look when it was finished. The Council had already chosen the words to be engraved above the door: "The fear of the Lord is the beginning of wisdom." It was a fitting verse, John thought. He dreamed of the scholars who would soon come to this building from all over the world to prepare to be ministers and evangelists in the service of the Lord Jesus Christ.

John had great plans for the "Academy," as he called it. There would be professors of Hebrew, Greek, philosophy, and theology. Theodore de Beza, whom John had met in Professor Wolmar's home, was a distinguished scholar now. He would serve as the first rector. John had also invited Professor Cordier to teach at the academy. The aged professor gladly accepted the invitation. John knew that his students would learn more than grammar from him. What long and great roads would lead from here?

A sudden desire seized John to visit one of the children's schools. He turned the corner and entered a plain building. John strode purposefully into the small classroom where students sat elbow to elbow to receive their lessons. He saw fresh enthusiasm for learning on the faces of the children. He remembered his own childhood and the hunger for knowledge that he had. "It is good," he murmured to himself. "This is how learning begins: small at first, and then it grows."

The teacher welcomed John, and several heads bobbed up. They recognized their pastor at once. "Let's show Pastor Calvin what you have learned," said the teacher. He began, "What is the inscription on the coat of arms of Geneva?"

The children answered in unison, "*Post tenebras lux.*"

"And what does it mean?" asked the teacher.

"After darkness, light."

"Why was this inscription chosen?"

Several children raised their hands. The teacher nodded to a tall, wiry boy. He stood and said, "Once the people of Geneva were in darkness, but now they have the light of the Bible."

JOHN AND THE CHILDREN

John complimented the children on their lessons. He thought about the boy's words. Truly, the light of God's Word was shining in Geneva. How important it was to teach this new generation so that they could be lights to people all over the world. As John left the building, he heard the children singing:

I greet Thee, Who my sure Redeemer art,

161

My only trust and Saviour of my heart,
Who pain didst undergo for my poor sake,
I pray Thee from our hearts all cares to take.
Thou art the King of mercy and of grace,
Reigning omnipotent in every place;
So come, O King, and our whole being sway;
Shine on us with the light of thy pure day.
Thou art the life by which alone we live
And all our substance and our strength receive,
Sustain us by thy faith and by thy power
And give us strength in every trying hour.
Our hope is in no other save in Thee;
Our faith is built upon thy promise free.
Lord, give us peace, and make us calm and
sure
That in thy strength we evermore endure.

John smiled as he recognized the words that he had written many years ago.

On Christmas Day, 1559, the man who had served Geneva for over twenty years was made a citizen of Geneva. Though John never requested the privilege, the people wanted to recognize the part he played in bringing the light of the Gospel to their city.

During the next few years John's health began to fail. He worked to finish several commentaries. He did not cease to preach, teach, counsel, and correspond with those who needed him, even on his death bed. When his friends begged him to rest, he declared, "Would you have the Lord find me idle when He comes?"

During John's last days, the pastors and leaders of Geneva visited him as he lay on his bed. Among them was Michel Cop, the younger brother of Nicholas Cop. He now served as pastor in Geneva. John told them, "Brethren, when I am dead, persevere in the work and be not dispirited."

He dictated a last letter to his dear friend, Farel. He wrote:

Geneva, 2nd May 1564

To Farel,

Farewell, my most excellent and upright brother . . . It is enough that I live and die for Christ, Who is to all his followers a gain both in life and death. Again I bid you and your brethren Farewell.

Faith and hope are the wings by which our souls,
rising above the world, are lifted up to God.

~ John Calvin

EPILOGUE

John Calvin was faithful as a servant to the people of Geneva. His successor, Theodore de Beza, said that John Calvin was a Christian Hercules who subdued so many monsters with the mightiest club of all, the Word of God.

Calvin contributed some of the most incisive and clear instructions on the Bible that have ever been written, both in his *Institutes of the Christian Religion* and in his many commentaries. He wrote commentaries on every book of the Bible except Song of Solomon and Revelation.

The Academy that he founded trained generations of pastors, teachers and evangelists who continued the work he had begun. One of its graduates, Casper Olevianus, was co-author of the Heidelberg Catechism. The Academy established the precedent for excellence in education which has influenced Protestant denominations all over the world.

Historians consider the roots of democracy

traceable to the pattern of church and civil government shaped by Calvin. He firmly believed that the church should be free from government control. John Adams, who was the second president of the United States, stated: "Let not Geneva be forgotten or despised. Religious liberty owes it most respect."

The historian George Bancroft wrote, "He that will not honor the memory and respect the influence of Calvin, knows but little of the origin of American liberty."

John served the Lord at a time when his knowledge of the Bible was desperately needed. Though he is considered one of the foremost leaders of the Reformation, Calvin resisted any special honors or recompense. He gave instructions at his death that his funeral and grave would be no different from the people he loved and served in life. Thus, he was buried without pomp in an unmarked grave. There is no monument over his grave to this day.

Yet, John Calvin is not forgotten. His tireless work to bring the truths of the Bible to all people endures through the legacy of believers all over the world who live by the light of the Bible that John and other Reformers helped to restore to a dark world. They served the Lord in the hope that His river of grace might enrich people everywhere.

OTHER FAMOUS PEOPLE MENTIONED IN THIS BOOK

Theodore de Beza
Rector of the Genevan Academy and successor to John Calvin in the church of Geneva

Martin Bucer
John's mentor in Strasbourg, Bucer was a leader of the Reformation in Germany. He worked to unite the Reformed and Lutheran branches of the Protestant church. He also assisted Archbishop Cranmer of England in bringing the Reformation to England.

Antoine Calvin
John's brother, who served as life-long assistant to John

Nicholas Cop
The son of the king's physician was rector of the Sorbonne University until he was deposed on account of his Protestant beliefs. His younger brother later served as pastor in the Genevan Church.

Mathurius Cordier
John dedicated his Commentary of I Thessalonians to this professor of Latin, and wrote:

> You were an instructor sent to me by God to teach me the true method of learning so that I might afterwards be a little more proficient. For me it was a singular kindness of God that I happened to have a propitious beginning to my studies. It is my desire to testify to posterity that, if they derive any profit from my writings, they should know that to some extent you are responsible for them.

Desiderius Erasmus
The gifted Greek scholar and leading humanist wrote *The Manual of the Christian Soldier*, and published the New Testament in Greek for the benefit of other scholars.

Lefevre d'Étaples
This Bible scholar led the early Reform movement in France, and influenced Martin Luther. He was charged with heresy and lived under the protection of Princess Margaret during his last years.

William Farel
This leader of the Reformation was a preacher in the Reform movement in France until he was exiled in 1523. He ministered in Geneva and later in Neuchatel, Switzerland.

Étienne de la Forge
The leader in the underground church in Paris was martyred for his faith during the Affair of the Placards.

King Francis I
The King of France fought unsuccessfully with Charles V, the Holy Roman Emperor. For a time King Francis was imprisoned in Madrid. He arranged the marriage of his son, Henry, to Catherine de Medici. Later, she used her influence over her royal sons to bring about the martyrdom of hundreds of Christians.

John Knox
Leader of the Reformation in Scotland, which resulted in the formation of the Presbyterian Church

Martin Luther
This leader of the Reformation translated the Bible into German, penned The Ninety-Five Theses which ignited the fires of Reformation, and wrote prolifically on behalf of the Gospel.

Princess Margaret d'Angouleme

Margaret was the sister of King Francis I and a defender of Protestants. Her legacy to France was her grandson, who became King Henry IV. He extended religious toleration to Protestants through the Edict of Nantes.

Philip Melanchthon

This associate of Martin Luther represented the German church at several councils, and was noted for his peace-keeping stance.

Pierre Robert or Olivétan

John's cousin was a translator of the Bible into French. He served the Waldensian Christians until his death at the age of 32.

Michael Servetus

Convicted as a heretic by the Catholic and Protestant churches, Servetus was the only heretic who died for his faith in Geneva.

Louis du Tillet

John's friend and canon in the church in Angouleme

Pierre Viret

One of John's closest friends, Viret was famous as a Reformer of Geneva and Lausanne, Switzerland.

William Whittingham

This member of the Genevan Church was the translator of the Geneva Bible, which was widely used by English-speaking Christians.

Melchior Wolmar

Noted Greek scholar and tutor of Theodore de Beza

BIBLIOGRAPHY

Calvin, John, Calvin: *Theological Treatises*, J. K. S. Reid, ed., (Philadelphia: Westminster Press, 1954)

Calvin, John, *Calvin's Commentary on Seneca's De Clementia*, translated by Ford Lewis Battles and Andre Malan Hugo, (Leiden: Renaissance Society of America, 1969)

Calvin, John, *Calvin's First Psalter*, edited by Richard R. Terry, (London: E. Benn, 1932)

Calvin, John, *Calvin's New Testament Commentaries*, 12 vols., David W. Torrance and Thomas F. Torrance, ed., (Grand Rapids: William B. Eerdmans, 1972)

Calvin, John, *The Deity of Christ and Other Sermons*, translated by Leroy Wilson, (Grand Rapids: Eerdmans, 1950)

Calvin, John, *Golden Booklet of the True Christian Life*, translated by Henry J. Van Andel, (Grand Rapids, MI: Baker Book House, 1952)

Calvin, John, *Institutes of the Christian Religion*, 2 vols., John T. McNeill, ed., Ford Lewis Battles, trans., (Philadelphia: The Westminster Press, 1960)

Calvin, John, *Instruction in Faith*, translated and edited by Paul T. Fuhrmann, (Philadelphia: Westminster Press, 1959)

Calvin, John, *Letters of John Calvin*, (Carlisle, PA: Banner of Truth Trust, 1980)

Calvin, John, *Selected Works of John Calvin: Tracts and Letters*, 7 vols., Henry Beveridge and Jules Bonnet, ed., (Grand Rapids: Baker Book House, 1983)

Calvin, John, *Tracts and Treatises*, With a Short Life of Calvin by Theodore Beza, translated by Henry Beveridge, (Grand Rapids: Eerdmans, 1958)

Christian History Magazine, Tuttle, Mark H., ed., "Meet Calvin" vol. V, no. 4 (Wheaton, IL: Christian History Institute, 1986)

Febvre, Lucien, edited and translated by Marian Rothstein, *Life in Renaissance France*, (Cambridge, MA: Harvard University Press, 1977)

Gerstner, Edna, *Idelette: A Novel based on the Life of Madame John Calvin*, (Morgan, PA: Soli Deo Gloria Publications, 1963)

McGrath, Alister E., *A Life of John Calvin*, (Oxford: Blackwell Publishers, 1990)

McNeill, John T., *The History and Character of Calvinism*, (Oxford: University Press, 1954)

Miller, J. Graham, *Calvin's Wisdom: An Anthology Arranged Alphabetically by a Grateful Reader*, (Carlisle, PA: Banner of Truth Trust, 1992)

Parker, T. H. L., *John Calvin: A Biography*, (Philadelphia: Westminster Press, 1975)

Renaissance, Reformation, and Absolutism, edited by Thomas G. Barnes and Gerald D. Feldman, (Boston: Little, Brown and Company, 1972)

Stepanek, Sally, *John Calvin* (New York: Chelsea House, 1986)

Stickelberger, Emanuel, *Calvin: A Life*, David Georg Gelzer, trans. (Richmond, Virginia: John Knox Press, 1954)

Van Halsema, Thea B., *This Was John Calvin*, (Grand Rapids, Michigan: Baker Book House, 1959)

HISTORY TITLES FROM GREENLEAF PRESS

BIOGRAPHIES BY JOYCE MCPHERSON
The Ocean of Truth: The Story of Sir Isaac Newton
A Piece of the Mountain: The Story of Blaise Pascal
Artist of the Reformation: The Story of Albrecht Dürer

THE FAMOUS MEN SERIES
Famous Men of Greece
Famous Men of Rome
Famous Men of the Middle Ages
Famous Men of the Renaissance and Reformation
Famous Men of the 16th & 17th Centuries

GREENLEAF GUIDES
The Greenleaf Guide to Old Testament History
The Greenleaf Guide to Ancient Egypt
The Greenleaf Guide to Famous Men of Greece
The Greenleaf Guide to Famous Men of Rome
The Greenleaf Guide to Famous Men of the Middle Ages
The Greenleaf Guide to Famous Men of the Renaissance and Reformation
The Greenleaf Guide to Famous Men of the 16th & 17th Centuries

Greenleaf Press carries over 1,500 titles -- Carefully selected living books from each period of history. Visit our website to request your copy of our complete catalog, or shop online at www.greenleafpress.com

Made in United States
Troutdale, OR
04/12/2024

19147538R00106